So, You Bought a Franchise. Now What?

So, You Bought a Franchise. Now What?

Dave Roemer

BUSINESS EXPERT PRESS

Leader in applied, concise business books

So, You Bought a Franchise. Now What?

Copyright © Business Expert Press, LLC, 2022.

Cover design by Charlene Kronstedt

DOI: 10.4128/9781637422724

Interior design by Exeter Premedia Services Private Ltd., Chennai, India

First published in 2022 by
Business Expert Press, LLC
222 East 46th Street, New York, NY 10017
www.businessexpertpress.com

ISBN-13: 978-1-63742-271-7 (paperback)
ISBN-13: 978-1-63742-272-4 (e-book)

Business Expert Press Entrepreneurship and Small
Business Management Collection

First edition: 2022

10 9 8 7 6 5 4 3 2 1

For Dottie. You are my inspiration, my life partner, my rock.

Description

This book is a practical guide to building a successful small business in general and a successful franchise business in specific. It provides best practices, tools, and practical knowledge that will help any small business achieve more success. It is specifically intended to help people who are franchisees of one of the thousands of franchise concepts out there, but the information contained within will help any small business owner. The author shares stories, proven best practices, and tools he has collected over more than 30 years working directly with franchisees and from being a franchisee himself. Included also are stories and advice from franchisees and operators who have built successful franchise businesses as well as business experts. Their contributions add to the practical nature of the information.

The reader does not need to read from beginning to end although it is certainly recommended you do. The book is designed so that if the reader needs help with one or two of the topics, he or she can read only those chapters or can read them at the point where the information is needed. The chapters are ordered to take the reader through the life cycle of his or her business from start to finish. It is the quintessential book on building a successful franchise business and with the growing number of people electing to become franchisees rather than employees, it could not have come at a better time.

Keywords

franchise; franchisee; franchise owner; small business; goal setting; local marketing; leadership; business success; business value; profitability; team building; customer loyalty; business growth; exit strategy

Contents

Testimonials

"There are many books out there about how to buy a franchise but few that are aimed at teaching the new franchisee how to get their foundation set in conjunction with the franchisors training. Dave has put together a masterful tome based on his decades of experience leading major brands. The knowledge that he shares is the same knowledge that has helped franchisees of major national brands grow their business and he offers it in an easy to read book that will leave you wanting more. Dave is the epitome of the American Dream and now he's paying it forward!"—**Nick Neonakis, CEO, The Franchise Consulting Company**

"David Roemer's—So, You Bought a Franchise, Now What? *is a must-read book for anyone who is contemplating buying a franchise, anyone who already owns a franchise or anyone whose business deals with the public. Mr. Roemer's approach is clear and concise and will truly help everyone to better understand the steps that will both enable and ensure their success. As a 45-year veteran of the franchise world—I wish I had Mr. Roemer's book 45 years ago."*—**Brian Zolotor, The Zolotor Consulting Group**

"Dave Roemer's book, So, You Bought a Franchise, Now What? *is a must read for anyone contemplating entry into the franchise arena. The tools and insights shared will prove invaluable in elevating the skills required for success. A superb read, both informational and transformational."*—**Bob Gershberg, CEO/Managing Partner, Wray Executive Search**

"Dave Roemer has a way to look inside the business different than most people."
—**Jim Sprick, Owner and President, Pinnacle Hospitality Group**

"Owing to Dave's comprehensive knowledge in the franchising industry this book will prove to be an essential asset when explaining what is good and bad when purchasing and developing a franchise, the quality of the franchise, the disciplines, the financial knowledge, the marketing support and the reporting protocols required. Franchises can, and do work, but tread carefully and

embrace a coach of Dave's calibre to help you."—**Stuart Allan, Stuart Allan and Associates**

"I'm very impressed with the way Dave presented this info. He did a great job of using a textbook approach and intermingling it with real life experience of those who have done it. I would recommend this to be a read for anyone who has gotten into a franchise but also if they are thinking about getting into a franchise."—**Carl Casalino, Owner, Bodkin Creek Foods, Next Gen Foods, Cross Country Ventures**

"Dave's unique insight goes well beyond which franchise system to select for individuals/investors. His insight and first-hand experiences drill down into the how and why franchisees often lose their way after they've selected and invested. Dave really sheds the light on how to be successful in ways that are teachable and tangible to the audience and reader. His decades of experience is why this is such a great read."—**David Ulrich, Principal, David Ulrich Associates**

"Dave's work on the real world, current blueprint to success when you buy a franchise is insightful and on-point. His awareness and shared processes that are outlined in the book are complete and well documented with his tremendous industry experience and his shared stories from many of his successful operators. It would be a terrific value for anyone that is searching for a roadmap to success."—**Greg Sausaman, CEO Topper's Creamery**

"I don't know anyone with more experience in training franchise business owners, consulting in all areas of their business and helping them keep their eye on the 'value' ball as they build their future."—**David Shavzin, Founder and President, The Value Track**

"If you are considering buying a franchise or improving a business you already own, Dave Roemer has written the book for you! Not only does Dave give priceless advice from his own experience running multiple franchises, he also introduces the reader to successful franchise owners with expertise specific to each chapter topic! This book is full of priceless conversations and wisdom! I highly recommend it!"—**Paul Reiser, President, Paul Reiser Companies**

"Dave Roemer's So, You Bought a Franchise, Now What? *provides the insights of his many years in company and franchise operations living, learning, and teaching the successful concepts outlined in this book. He has also brought together many operators from diverse industries who share their perspective on key areas of the business you must focus on to succeed. Dave hits the key elements to starting, operating, managing, and planning for long term growth along with the conclusion of an exit strategy. The book is a quick read that doesn't get put down. "*—**Bob Hill, Franchise Industry Professional**

Acknowledgments

There are several people I want to acknowledge as this book would not have been possible with them. First to all those who contributed, both franchisees and experts alike. To Stephen Robles who through his example of kindness and genuineness inspired me to be a better person. To Cindy Gray and Lynn Givens who I never met in person but were kind enough to give me some of their precious time and answer the questions of a stranger, thank you. To the other people who spent in some cases over an hour sharing their stories, Jim Sprick, Jim Sill, Carl Casalino, and Bob Hill, I cannot thank you enough for your graciousness and friendship.

To Greg Sausaman, who encouraged me and supported me through his words and his example. When we worked together all those years ago, you pushed me to do better and be better. You may not know it but you are still doing that today. Thank you my friend.

To Paul Reiser whom I have also only met on Zoom, thank you so much for your incredible insights and sharing your experience. But mostly, thank you for responding to my LinkedIn message. It's funny how life puts the right people in our path at the right time. You were absolutely the person I needed at the time I needed you.

To David Shavzin and Mark Fonseca, thank you both. We have only known each other for a short period of time and only over Zoom meetings but I have come to respect you both through what you have shared in those meetings. That is why I asked you to contribute and was confident you would say yes. I very much appreciate you for adding to these pages. And I must add a thank you to Jim Weber, the founder of ITB partners. Were it not for you Jim, I would never have met David and Mark.

To David Fisher and Mahesh Patel. You did not know I was including your stories, so I thank you for allowing me to keep them in. You are both good friends and my life is richer for knowing you. Mahesh, we need to get on the course soon and Dave, I miss our Saturday morning breakfasts.

To the unidentified people in some of my stories, thank you for allowing me to learn from you.

To Stuart Allan, my brother from another mother, thank you for your time and contribution. I cannot tell you how much it means to be able to catch up periodically with you from across the pond. You are the best stiff-assed Brit in the world.

To Rick Cooper my other brother from another mother, who would have known we would become such good friends when we first met. I have you to thank for that since you took the lead as you usually do with everything in your life. You have helped me in ways I cannot begin to express and I know the scale leans a lot more toward my side. I owe you more than I can ever repay.

To Nigel Wyatt and the folks at Business Expert Press. Thank you for taking a chance on an unknown aspiring author with an idea. I could not have gotten this book to market without you taking that chance, so thank you.

And to my wife Dottie, you are the reason for this happening at all. During my darkest times, you are my light. It was at one of those times that you said to me, "Now you have time to write that book" and told me over and over that I could do it. You believed in me when I did not believe in myself. You pushed me to do what I thought impossible. Thank you for putting up with me and sticking by me when I did not make it easy to do either. You are the love of my life.

Introduction

Congratulations! You bought a franchise and you are now a business owner. No longer are you subject to the whims and desires of a boss who can decide to eliminate your position or replace you with someone younger and cheaper. You are now in complete control of your future success.

The question you need to answer is "Now what?" If you are like many other new franchisees, you have never owned a business until now. You are undoubtedly excited and probably a bit terrified. Not to worry, that is completely natural. Hopefully, you learned some valuable lessons going through the due diligence process and deciding which franchise was best for you. One thing you probably learned is that having trusted advisers is critical. Your accountant and attorney gave you great advice and will continue to do so. Fellow franchisees can also be a great source of advice and wisdom. Fellow franchisees do not always have a lot of time as they are busy running their own business.

I have been fortunate in my career that I have been surrounded by some very smart people. I am also fortunate that I had the good sense (most of the time) to listen to those people and learn as much as I could from them. I have also been in some situations where I had to learn or I was doomed.

My first great learning experience in business came when I operated a 24-hour seven day a week business. We closed only one day a year, Christmas Day. That first Christmas I operated that business, I realized there was no key for the door and had to get a locksmith to re-key the lock. Fortunately, I did not wait until Christmas to look for the key. That business required a lot of what you will find in this book, a vision, people skills, a keen eye for numbers, and a lot of hard work. Fortunately, I was young and did not mind hard work. The rest I had to learn as I went.

One of the main lessons I learned, you will read about in Chapter 3, which is to constantly be training team members. By the way, your people are team members not employees. Having the mindset that people are your employees makes them subservient and puts them automatically in a lower position than you. I will talk more about that in Chapter 3, but understand that is why this paragraph is the only place you will see the word "employees" unless it is part of a direct quote from one of my contributors.

So, training became a passion of mine early on and I was fortunate to work in the Dunkin' Donuts training department for five years. During that time, I trained hundreds of newly signed Dunkin' franchisees how to effectively operate a Dunkin'. I learned a lot, yet I did not realize how much I still had to learn.

After that stint in the training department, in 1989 I was sent into the field to work with franchisees as a business consultant. That began the more than 30-year journey, which has led to writing this book. During those 30-plus years, I have worked with franchisees who owned one location and franchisees who have owned as many as 85 locations. I found I had a love and a knack for coaching franchisees to be more successful. Many had never before owned a business and had to learn how to think like an owner. Most of those never had a team and needed to learn how to hire, train, and retain great people. Being in a position of coach and consultant kept me on my toes and forced me to learn so I could stay at least one step ahead of my franchisees. I realized I needed more education so I went back to school and got a degree in business and then an MBA. What that did for me more than anything was get me back into reading books.

I have found reading to be the best education I could ever have. Reading has allowed me to learn from some of the greatest business executives and thought leaders in business over the past 40 years. Reading has given me the equivalent of taking graduate level courses from Ken Blanchard, Peter Drucker, Stephen Covey, Jim Collins, Simon Sinek, Zig Ziglar, Dale Carnegie, Larry Bossidy, John Maxwell, and many others. I strongly suggest you look up these names and read everything you can by them.

In 2013, after years of working with franchisees, I decided to become one myself. I bought a small business coaching franchise because it seemed like the perfect marriage between coaching small business owners and being a franchisee. I did that just over two years and it was the greatest learning experience of my life. My coaching skills improved exponentially and I learned more about myself than at any other time in my life. Unfortunately, I ran out of money before I could get the business where I needed it and so I had to give it up. That also was an incredible learning experience albeit a painful one.

The past few years I have been back working with franchisees to help them grow and achieve their dreams. The difference has been that I have had the chance to lead teams of franchise coaches and help them better serve their franchisees too. For me, the more business owners I can impact in a positive way, the happier I am so this work was a blast.

Today, I help people find the right franchise opportunity for them. My approach is to learn as much as possible about the person and then find a franchise brand that is a good fit for their skills, finances, lifestyle, and purpose in life. It is interesting work and allows me time for my other love, writing.

Your franchisor can provide you with help and many of the good ones do. Again, there are limits to that. Franchisor advice tends to be mainly around the technical aspects of the business because that is their area of expertise. Sometimes a franchisor has someone able to give you more general business-oriented advice. Again it can be limited as it depends on the person giving it. If, like me and others I have known through the years, your field representative is passionate about helping people succeed and understands what it takes to run a successful business, then you are fortunate. If not, well, that's why I wrote this book.

According to the website statista.com, in 2019 there were 7,73,603 franchise establishments in the United States.[1] Every day, hundreds or even thousands of people sign up to be a franchisee of one of the thousands of franchise brands throughout the world. Many of them are first-time business owners who are not fully prepared for the realities of business ownership. They depend on the franchisor to help them. Most, if not all, franchisors provide support for their franchisees preopening and for a short time postopening. The better franchisors provide some level of support on the technical aspects of operating the business throughout the term of the franchise agreement. The amount of ongoing support

---

[1] H. Ward. 2020. "Number of Franchise Establishments in the United States From 2007 to 2020". Franchise industry: number of establishments U.S. 2019 | Statista, July 18, 2021.

a typical franchisee receives however, has diminished as franchisors face increased pressure on their own profitability.

If franchisors are not helping their franchisees with the technical aspects of the business, they are certainly not helping franchisees with the more generic aspects of business ownership. Things such as goal setting, hiring great people, leadership, local marketing, managing their finances, building customer loyalty, and increasing business value are things franchisors tell their franchisees they must do but are largely unwilling or unable to help them accomplish.

Help is finally here. In these pages are a host of stories about what successful franchisees did to achieve success. There are tools to help you execute procedures that have a proven record of working. There is also plenty of inspiration to give you the courage to push forward and overcome whatever obstacles are in the way.

This book is designed primarily for franchisees no matter the brand but the lessons within will also help any independent small business owner. In the pages that follow, I will share my more than 30 years of expertise in working with small business owners to work ON their business rather than IN their business as well as my own experience as a franchisee. Through the years, I formed strong relationships with many of those owners. Several of the more successful ones were interviewed and their stories and advice are an integral part of this book. What better way to learn how to operate a successful small business than by listening to other successful owners talk about how they became successful.

If this book helps you even in some small way, then I have accomplished my mission. It has been said that those who can, do. Those who can't, teach. I would add those who can do both, write a book. I hope you not only enjoy this book, but you also gain some practical knowledge and are able to put that knowledge to use in achieving your dreams. And don't forget to have fun along the way. I wish you success, joy, and happiness in all you do.

CHAPTER 1

What Is Your Purpose?

Profit isn't a purpose, it's a result. To have purpose means the things we do are of real value to others.

—Simon Sinek

I have asked hundreds of business owners over the years this question: "Why did you get into this business?" The answers of course vary from owner to owner and are usually some form of "To provide for my family," or "To make a good living," or even "To be my own boss." Making more money and working for yourself are great reasons for going into business. What I learned though was that the owners who got into business for the sole purpose of making money, never made much. Certainly not as much as they could have made. And the ones who wanted to work for themselves, while happy, were not always fulfilled.

Put another way, your purpose is WHY you do something; goals are HOW you do it.

In a Facebook video on February 25, 2021, Ken Blanchard said "A purpose, a why statement is not a goal. A goal has a beginning and an end. A why statement is why are you doing this?" Your purpose or your why keeps you on the path you set from the beginning. If you ever stray from that path, reviewing your purpose immediately gets you back on track.

In his book, "Start With Why,"[1] author Simon Sinek writes that people don't buy what you do or how you do it, they buy why you do it. People want to be part of something, a member of the club. That's why people are so loyal to Apple they will wait online overnight to get the newest iPhone on the day it is released.

---

[1] S. Sinek. n.d. *Start With Why*, 41. USA: Penguin Group.

Apple started as a computer company but today it is better described as an electronics company. Why has the public essentially permitted Apple to successfully introduce and sell such a diversified array of products? The answer is that people don't buy what Apple does, they buy why they do it. Apple's original mission statement was:

> To make a contribution to the world by making tools for the mind that advance humankind[2]

Nothing in there about making the best products or providing the best service or even about making computers. That mission statement is clearly about wanting to change the world and making it easier for people to expand their knowledge for the benefit of the human race. It's pretty easy to see why people would connect with and rally around that.

On a personal level, the reason I wrote this book had nothing to do with money. Do I hope it sells some copies and I make some money from it? Of course I do. Probably not as much as my publisher but still, I hope so. My purpose for writing this book is about my WHY. After years of soul searching and hundreds of attempts to write down my WHY, I finally came up with this:

> I help people be more knowledgeable and skillful than the yesterday version of themselves so that they are better positioned to realize their dreams.

While it has only been in recent years that I have been able to voice that purpose, I realize that it has been driving me for most of my career. Early on, I was completely driven by money. That's why I left college without a diploma and went to work full time at Dunkin' Donuts. I saw my friends graduating with a diploma getting jobs for $12,000 per year. When I was promoted to store manager, I was paid a salary of $18,000 per year. My decision to leave school was instantly justified. Then as a store manager, I was sent to a manager certification course. It was during

---

[2] June 02, 2009. "Mission Statement," *The Economist*.

those three weeks of training, after watching the trainers, that I realized I wanted to be a trainer too. That was when I first began to realize my calling as a teacher and coach.

Later I began working directly with franchisees as a franchise coach. I was responsible for making sure that franchisees understood and followed systems and standards. More importantly, I was tasked with helping them improve sales, service, hiring, and profitability. In essence, my job was to help franchisees be more successful. After a short time, I began realizing I really enjoyed seeing franchisees become more successful and knowing I had a small role in helping them get there. I felt like I had found my purpose in life. Over the years, I have never felt more fulfilled than when I see a franchisee achieve a goal that really mattered to him or her and know that I was there through the entire process of setting the goal and cheering the franchisee on every step of the way. To me, that is worth more than any amount of money or bonus I have earned.

Practical Reasons for Discovering Your WHY

Stephen Robles is a multiunit franchisee of Long John Silver's. I have spoken with Stephen often in the years we have known each other about his purpose for starting his company Whitestone Foods. I had the privilege of speaking with Stephen for over an hour in preparation for this writing. The quotes that follow are from that interview.

In over 12 years as a franchisee, Stephen has seen good times and tough times. His business has been up and it has been down. Through it all, Stephen believes that what has sustained him and his organization through the bad times is being driven by a purpose. When I asked Stephen about this he said:

I've gone through some challenges and we all do in business. It can be anything from bad sales to people getting sick or whatever but what I've found is that because I am purpose driven and my organization understands what we stand for, we lock arms and work together to get things done.

Stephen's WHY is very simple:

To Make Others Rich

On the surface, it appears Stephen is driven to make others financially wealthy. While money is part of it, Stephen is more concerned with making people rich spiritually and emotionally. One example Stephen gave me was the story of one of his people who emigrated from Syria and whose elderly mother still lived there. This team member would be gone for a month at a time visiting his mother before she passed away. Stephen was happy he could help make that team member rich with memories before his mother passed.

Another story Stephen told me was of a team member with five children who came to work for him. For some time she was the definition of an excellent team member. She worked hard, her work quality was excellent, and she fit well into the company culture. All of a sudden, things changed. Her work fell off dramatically. In many companies, she would have been given a written warning and let go if her work did not improve but not at Whitestone Foods. Stephen sensed something was wrong at home and when he asked her about it, he found out his intuition was correct. Stephen listened to her story and supported her emotionally and spiritually. He enriched her life with love for another human being, which helped her get through a difficult time. As Stephen said to me:

> If I can create an environment that enriches you as a person, I'm all about that. I could have just probably fired her and just been like most businesspeople, it's all performance based, you're not cutting it, you're gone. But when I hired her, she was a mom with five kids. She did corporate tax, undergrad degree in accounting, graduated Suma Cum Laude with five kids. She's just a rock star. My goal was to make her rich, to give her exposure to the kind of accounting we do. It's pretty simple accounting that we do, but I wanted to invest in her. So that became my little voice, you know? You've got to make her rich. I want the best fed, most loved employees in any industry and so that becomes what keeps me going everyday.

I don't want to make Stephen out to be an entirely selfless person. Like you and me, he is not. Here is how he puts it:

If I can do all that (make others rich), hopefully I've built an organization that looks at other people, right? And part of that is how do I make Stephen rich? Again, it's not about money. How do I take care of Stephen? That becomes why we do things. I'm making others rich by feeding them. That's why I get up every day.

Another way his WHY plays out in everyday life is that Stephen's people are comfortable with letting him know when he is not living up to the principles he preaches. Stephen told me that one day he was scheduled to do a performance review with one of his best general managers. The guy ran a great store with positive sales growth, positive profits growth, lived the values, and so on, but because of COVID-19 there was concern about doing anything face to face. Here is how Stephen told the story:

> I want to get his review done. And I was going to do it over the phone. I got a phone call from Hanano (district manager) who said I hope you don't take this wrong, but I just don't think you should do a review over the phone. I would just wait and just do a face to face because it just means so much more to them when you sit down with them face to face. It doesn't align with our values, does it? No, it doesn't align with our values. And so I was being kind of checked by one of my people who had the confidence, I guess he felt the freedom to tell me, that, hey, you know what, you're not living your values, you know, you're not really loving on the people. If you really loved them, you would sacrifice, get in your car drive three and a half hours, sit down with them, love on them and show some appreciation. So I said you know what, you're right. You're absolutely right. So I got to get up early to make the drive.

The other thing he told me was, "The biggest test for having a purpose beyond making money is your employees." He said, "Your employees can smell when you're more dollar driven versus purpose driven." The point is that no matter what business you're in or how large or small your business is, to be successful you must connect with people on something that matters to them.

So how can you determine your purpose and boil it down to a clear statement? Like most worthwhile endeavors the process, while uncomplicated, will require time and effort. It starts with a trip down memory lane.

Finding Your WHY

When I had my coaching franchise, I had the privilege of helping a client discover his WHY. Dave Fisher is a financial consultant who today works mainly with small business owners. When I first met Dave, he had two jobs in 15 months and was bagging groceries at Whole Foods. He had been searching for a few years for a career that filled his soul, not just his pockets. He called me one day and said that he thought he made a decision and could we meet for coffee. I, of course, said sure!

The first thing Dave said to me was that he decided to become a financial planner. He said he felt like he could help people by helping them plan for retirement and improve their financial lives.

To find his WHY, Dave and I followed the method outlined in Simon Sinek's sequel "Find Your Why."[3] First, he drew a horizontal line on a piece of paper. Then he went back in his memory and identified the events, good or bad, that had the most impact on him. The good memories he noted on top of the line and the bad ones below the line. The events that had the most impact he wrote further away from the line so that the highest impact memories were the furthest from the line. Then on another page, he wrote a few lines about each memory to describe it. As you can imagine, this can be a very emotional experience. I recommend completing this task alone as it may stir up feelings you are not yet ready to share. You also want to be free to allow things to come to you and sort out the feelings in the next step.

Once Dave had his list of high impact memories, it was time for us to meet. Keep in mind, we had set this up beforehand. I also had some homework to complete about how to best help Dave sort through his memories, how each made him feel, how strong his feeling were and why he had those feelings. It's important to note here that while Dave and

---

[3] S. Sinek. 2017. *Find Your Why: A Practical Guide for Finding Purpose for You and Your Team.* New York, NY: Portfolio/Penguin.

I had a mainly professional relationship, the most important factor was trust. Dave trusted me enough to hear his private stories, not judge him and ask questions to help him dig deeper into why these particular memories were so vivid and impactful on his life. The key for me to being a good partner in the endeavor was listening and staying focused on helping Dave achieve greater understanding.

As I asked questions, most of which started with the word *why*, Dave began to get clearer about why these memories had so much impact on him. He started realizing that the good memories all revolved around times when he was either part of a group that was involved with something meaningful or around people who were working toward a common goal. These were the times when he was happiest. He also realized that he was unhappiest when he was stuck in chaos and everyone was working at cross purposes. Out of all that came his WHY:

To bring people together around a common cause so that all achieve their heart's desire.

As a financial consultant, Dave now fulfills his purpose by talking with people about what is important to them, their heart's desire. So if he is talking with a married couple, he first finds out what they want most in life. This requires Dave to ask a lot of questions and find the couple's common cause. Sometimes it happens that the couple thought they were on the same page but are not. In those cases, Dave will take a step back and try to help them discover a common cause. If he cannot, he will advise the clients to work on it and get back to him. That's how much he believes in the first part of his WHY.

When Dave is able to help his clients voice their common cause or heart's desire, which is most of the time, he then helps them build a financial plan that will allow them to achieve their heart's desire. Today Dave is more successful financially than ever and more important, he is happier and more fulfilled than ever. He has found what for him is the perfect way to earn a living by achieving his own heart's desire.

I cannot stress enough the importance of finding your why. Ideally, you will have done it before you purchased your franchise business. The likelihood though is that you did not. That doesn't make you a bad business owner or even a bad person for that matter. It does put you in a category of most business owners who jump into business without really understanding the true reason why. You may have an inkling of why but if you are like the rest of us, you have not taken the time to look deep and figure out the real reason you are so driven to succeed in business.

Don't waste another day without knowing your WHY. Start the process today. It may take you a while to figure it out but if you start today, you will know your WHY one day earlier than if you start tomorrow. Everything you do in business or in life will be determined by your WHY. Every correct decision you make will align with your WHY. Every goal you set, every person you hire, all your marketing, how you read and evaluate your financial statements will be based on your WHY.

My hope for you is that you find your purpose beyond simply making money. I also hope that you use your franchise business as a vehicle to fulfill your purpose. As I said earlier, making money is important. I want you to make a lot of money and use it to fund the achievement of your life's purpose. The remaining chapters are designed to give you the tools and materials you will need to build a successful business and achieve your purpose; so buckle up, because here we go.

CHAPTER 2

Setting Goals

Our goals can only be reached through a vehicle of a plan, in which we must fervently believe, and upon which we must vigorously act. There is no other route to success.

—Pablo Picasso

Now that we have talked about WHY you bought your business, let's talk about HOW you will achieve success. This chapter is the foundation of everything that follows. If you master the skills outlined here, you are more than halfway to your promised land.

Setting goals, when done effectively, is a process. As Mr. Picasso said, achieving success is a function of creating a plan in which you have absolute belief and then taking action. That last part, taking action, is where most of us fall down.

Here is the good news, setting goals is not a particularly complicated process. In fact, it is really not that difficult. The difficulty lies in taking consistent action and holding yourself accountable. It takes a lot of discipline to achieve your goals. Fortunately, once you get into the groove, achieving your goals is so fulfilling it almost becomes addictive.

Early in my career, setting goals was completely foreign to me. I was given targets to hit but I had no say in establishing them and no one ever talked to me about what my personal goals were. Even growing up there was no talk about setting and achieving goals. Anything resembling that subject was always very vague and undefined. As a result, I was extremely unfocused and had no clue what I wanted to do with my life. The closest I had to a goal was to get a good job and make a good living.

It wasn't until 1996 that I set my first true goal to achieve a specific result. I was 37 years old at the time. Understand, I had been reasonably successful in life and in my career up until then. I had received several promotions and raises at work. I was married with two beautiful daughters;

we owned a home (with the bank) and were part of a community. Things were going well but that feeling of being unfocused and having no real purpose was always there. I was letting everything happen to me rather than making things happen.

So, in 1996 I decided to go back to school and get a degree in business. For the first time in my life, I had a goal. Not only was I going to get the degree but I was also going to get an A in every course. My company would reimburse me 100 percent of the tuition for every A grade but only 75 percent for a B and 50 percent for a C. So I made it my mission to achieve an A every time. And so with the unwavering support of my wife, I achieved my goal. I also achieved something even greater; I realized for the first time that if I set a specific target that focused my effort and actions, I could achieve anything. In fact, once I achieved that goal I had so much momentum that again with my wife's unwavering support, I kept it going and ended up with an MBA.

At this point, I still did not know anything about the goal-setting process. It was not until several years later, when I was in my mid-forties, that I learned about setting SMART goals, visualizing and action plans. That was when it started coming together. I say starting to come together because a few years later I learned how to zero in on my priorities, accelerate the process, and really start to make things happen. So, let's dig in and talk about the best way I know of to set and achieve goals.

SMART Goals

You may have heard the term SMART goals. SMART is an acronym for:

Specific
Measurable
Attainable
Realistic
Timebound

In short, if your goals are not written down and do not contain these five characteristics, they are not goals, they are dreams. Don't get me wrong, dreams are great. It's just that goals are more motivating and drive you to take action. It is in the action that goals are achieved.

Let's understand what each of these characteristics means and why it's important.

Specific

The target must be clearly defined so there is no question as to what it is. Being specific creates accountability while being fuzzy allows you to not feel so bad when you fail to hit it. Specificity creates accountability as well as fear of failure. If the goal matters to you, and if it doesn't why set it, then defining success and failure are important motivators that only have meaning when the target is specific.

For example, let's say your goal is:

Increase Sales

Is it specific? No, it is not. Increasing sales is certainly a good thing to do but how much will you increase sales? Over what time period and as compared to what time period? It's a fuzzy goal that leaves too much room for excuses. Will this goal motivate your team? Can you set up a reward system that makes sense for you and them? If you answer yes to those questions, we need to have a serious conversation so call me.

What if you want a new car? Would you write the goal to read "Buy a new car"? Of course not. Have you ever wanted just any new car? Sure, maybe initially you say you want a new car but then you start looking around and decide what make and model you want, how much you want to spend, what features it has, and so on. Then you set the goal of getting that particular car with those particular features at that particular price. You probably also find a picture of it so you can point and say "That's the car I am going to get." That is a specific goal.

Measurable

How will you know when you hit the target if you can't measure the result? This ties pretty closely with being specific but narrows the focus considerably. A runner doesn't aim to run faster, she or he aims for a particular time because that can be measured. Being measurable allows you to determine how close you are to your goal and so how much harder you need to work to get there. I will talk more about this later and share some research that proves the point. For now though, is this goal measurable?

Increase Sales by 5 Percent

On the surface, it appears to be measurable and it certainly is better than the previous example. It's close but not quite there. If you are going to increase sales by 5 percent, you need a time period and a base period for comparison. What period will you use to measure current sales and what period will you use to compare it to? Even if you eliminated the percent increase and used a specific amount instead, you would still need to define the period in order to measure success or failure.

Attainable

Is the goal something you can accomplish in the given time period? Given the resources you have to use in attaining this goal, can you do it? In the case of a 5 percent increase in sales, it doesn't sound like a very large number. For some businesses it may be too large to attain, while in others it may be an easy number to hit. It would certainly seem attainable for most companies. Spending a modest amount of money on advertising or creating a special incentive will likely get you an increase of 5 percent.

Don't sell yourself or your team short here. In your quest to make sure you set attainable goals, don't shorten your reach. Attainable doesn't mean the goal should take little or no effort to reach. Goals should challenge you and your team but not be impossible either. Too easy and you will feel empty when you achieve it. Any celebration will ring hollow and your team will not be fooled either. Too hard and the hopelessness of being able to hit the goal will be de-motivating. Over time it builds resentment and everyone just gives up. Set the goal just beyond your reach so you have to stretch a little to get there.

Realistic

Is the goal realistic within the context of your WHY as well as your annual goals? The goal needs to fit with everything else you are trying to achieve. On the surface, it would certainly seem like increasing sales fits with everything and I would say it does. The 5 percent piece may not fit though. Let's say that the year before was a particularly bad year and sales were down 20 percent for the quarter. Maybe there was road construction in front of your business that is now complete and no longer an issue. A mere 5 percent increase this year would be unrealistic.

Assume that two years ago your sales for the quarter were $100,000. A 20 percent decrease would mean that last year sales were $80,000. This year the construction is no longer a factor; so, if you got back to $100,000 where you were two years ago it would be a 25 percent increase over last year because you are doing the math on a smaller base. In this context it would seem 5 percent is not realistic. First it may be too small a goal, which you would find yourself adjusting upward after only a couple of weeks. Second, you may need to get all the way back to $100,000 to generate enough profit to achieve other goals you set. Maybe you had to take money from savings to survive the previous year and that meant you couldn't donate to that charity you love.

Remember that new car you wanted? Does it fit with your WHY? Does driving a Hummer H2 fit with your WHY of reducing global warming? Probably not. Maybe you should wait until 2023 when Hummer is expected to introduce an electric vehicle.

Timebound

Setting a deadline is an absolute must. Goals are not the same as a purpose. A purpose is an ideal that you strive to reach over a lifetime knowing that you will never quite get there. Goals are achievable aims that get you closer to fulfilling your purpose. Without a deadline to work toward, a goal is meaningless. With a deadline you will work hard to reach your goal. You may even move mountains and surprise yourself in the process. You never know what you can achieve until you set a SMART goal and then work with determination to achieve it.

So, with all that, here are some examples of goals written in a SMART way:

Increase sales by five percent for Q4 2021 compared to the same quarter last year

Buy a navy blue 2022 BMW M3 with 20 percent down by March 1, 2022

These are SMART goals. They are specific in that we know exactly what the targets are. We want to increase sales by 5 percent in Q4 2021 over Q4 2020. We want to purchase not just a BMW; we want a blue M3 and we want to have 20 percent down payment.

They are measurable in that we will know exactly if we have achieved them.

They certainly seem attainable assuming we can save the 20 percent down payment in the prescribed time given the amount we need and our income level.

I think it is safe to say that a 5 percent sales increase for any business is realistic and relevant. As for the BMW purchase, who is to say it is not a realistic goal?

Finally, the goals are time bound. There are specific timeframes to achieve both goals with deadlines so we can measure if we have achieved the goal or not.

I mentioned earlier that I was in my mid-forties when I first learned a process for setting and achieving goals. I was working for Arby's at the time and my boss thought we needed a training session on how to set goals. He was right, of course. He had some folks from the training department who taught us about SMART goals and then had us create goal boards using a process I describe in the next section. It was very enlightening for me and I have continued to use elements of the process I learned that day. I say elements because I have since learned more about setting goals and have refined my process using pieces of everything I learned that I found work the best.

Before I share this refined process for setting and achieving goals, I think it's important to explain some things about why this process works. These things have to do with human physiology and psychology and how the brain works. Understand however that I am not an expert in either human physiology or psychology. I am a lay person who has done some reading on the topics as they relate to goal setting and applied my personal logic and common sense. If you want a deeper understanding of these two topics, you will need to find it elsewhere.

The Physiology and Psychology of Goal Setting

I'm not going to bore you with a lot of scientific and psychological mumbo jumbo, but I think it's important for you to understand why SMART goals and the process I will outline in this chapter are important. Understanding why something is important makes you more likely to diligently follow the process. Remember, people don't buy what you do or how you do it. They buy why you do it. The same principle follows here.

First, as a logical, thinking human being we all understand that having something to aim for increases the chances of hitting it. Jordan Peterson a professor of psychology at the University of Toronto says "One of the things you can be virtually certain of in life is that you don't hit something you don't aim at."[1] Seems pretty logical to me. Robin Hood never would have split that arrow if he didn't aim at it.

When you aim at a target and hit it your brain releases a chemical called dopamine, which gives you a feeling of pleasure. This is your body's reward system. Dopamine is meant to make you feel good and the fact that it is released immediately upon achieving a goal creates a strong behavioral association. That makes you want to set and achieve another goal so you can get that good feeling again. This is also why setting short-term goals, as you will see later, is much more effective than only setting long-term goals. The longer the wait between releases of dopamine, the less effective it is as a reward. Dopamine is the habit-forming chemical in your brain and the reason why when you do something regularly at short intervals you keep doing it.

Another important tool to goal achievement is visualization, which has both physiological and psychological element to it. By visualizing

---

[1] J. Peterson. 2018. "How to Set Goals the Smart Way". www.youtube.com/watch?v=5WX9UEYZsR8&t=3s

yourself succeeding, you fool your brain into thinking you've achieved your goal already and it releases some dopamine. Yes, it is tricky.

The psychological aspect works a bit differently.

Have you ever bought a new car and all of a sudden you notice the same make and model everywhere as you drive down the road? Ever said to yourself after buying a Ford Taurus for example, "Wow, I never realized there are so many Taurus models on the road?"

The reason you are noticing so many Taurus models is because your reticular activating system or RAS is now focused on your new Taurus. Your RAS is a series of neurons in your brain that filters out unnecessary stuff, which allows you to focus only on what's important. When you buy a new car, you're excited and thinking a lot about it as you drive down the road. Your RAS filters out, unconsciously of course, the cars around you and zeros in on the ones like yours.

Athletes are taught to visualize because it trains their RAS to filter out failure and focus on success. When standing on the free throw line, professional basketball players visualize the ball going in the basket. That visualization not only increases the odds of making the point, it filters out all the noise and distractions created by the fans and other players designed to make them miss. Golfers also visualize their shots going down the middle of the fairway or in the hole because it filters out everything else like water, sand, and the rough.

When I teach people how to set and achieve goals, one of the things I do is have them create goals boards. As part of the preparation process, I have my boxes of old magazines and tell the attendees to bring as many magazines as they can find. It doesn't matter what it is. Any magazine will do. In this way, we always end up with an excellent assortment. Everyone in the class gets a poster board, pair of scissors, and a glue stick. As you'll see later, this is an important step near the end of the goal-setting process. Participants find pictures representing their goals in the magazines, cut them out, and paste them to the poster board. Each one in turn presents their board to the group to make a verbal commitment and increase their accountability. The board then receives a prominent place in the office or home where it will be seen often thus building that filter in the RAS.

Visualization is a powerful tool in the setting and achieving of goals. Jack Niklaus who is arguably the greatest golfer who ever lived has been quoted as saying "I never hit a shot, even in practice, without having a very sharp in-focus picture of it in my head." Here is what I know:

1. Writing down my goals and having visual reminders that I see often has helped me achieve goals.
2. I have worked with clients who previously never set goals who have used visualization and the process I am about to explain to achieve things in their business they had never thought possible.

Whether or not there are statistics to support these facts is irrelevant. I have seen the process work over and over with individuals and teams. If you and your team want to begin reaching new heights of achievement and have fun in the process, here is how you do it.

The Goal-Setting Process

Now that you know how to write SMART goals, let's talk about how you decide what you want to accomplish and how you go about getting that done. The process for setting and achieving your goals is straightforward and uncomplicated. One other note, if you choose to set personal goals in addition to business goals, the process is the same.

The first decision to make in the goal-setting process is the time period for which you will set your goals. I suggest you set goals for three periods of time, five years, one year, and 90 days. Your five-year goals should seem like they are almost impossible to achieve. Yes, I know the R in SMART stands for realistic but I also know I said almost impossible. A five-year goal should be a super stretch goal and really challenge you. It should be something that should scare you a little. If it's a bit scary it will force you to set better yearly and quarterly goals and be excited about hitting those. Also, set no more than three five-year goals. A basic principle of goal setting is, less is more. Having too many goals causes you to lose focus. I prefer no more than two but for a five-year period, three is OK.

Your one-year or annual goals will support achieving your five-year goals. For example, if you want to reach $1 million in sales in five years, your annual goals need to realistically get you there.

At this point, I have not mentioned anything beyond the writing of goals. While having your goals written down in SMART form is a critical first step, that alone will not get you where you want to be. The real power of goal setting is in the specific action steps you take to achieve your goals and that happens every 90 days.

Setting 90-day or quarterly goals, adding action steps and defining who is accountable for each step is the secret to releasing the power of goal setting. Remember our friend dopamine? This is where that reward chemical comes into play and the magic of goal setting happens. Ninety days is a time frame that you can keep in constant sight. It is long enough to give you the time needed to accomplish something meaningful and short enough to always see the end point. It also allows you to set short-term actions steps that give you frequent shots of dopamine, which maintains your motivation and creates momentum.

Actually, there is a second secret to releasing the power of goal setting; focus on no more than two goals each quarter. The temptation to focus on a lot of goals will be great. Do not fall prey to it. It's fine to start with a list of things you want to accomplish in any 90-day period, and to be sure you end up with the one or two most important goals you will start out with a list of 5 or 10. As you will see, there is a tool that will help you whittle your list down to the most important two.

If you have some key people on your team, you will want them to be part of creating your 90-day plan. They will help you achieve the plan so they should help you create it. Having buy-in from your key team members is important. What follows is the process for setting quarterly goals. I follow this process and have taught many others this same process. It has been used by hundreds or even thousands of business owners to achieve their 90-day goals.

90-Day Goal-Setting Process

1. Review one-year and five-year goals.
2. Determine where you need to be in 90 days in the following areas:
   a. Finances
      i. Sales
      ii. Costs
      iii. Profit
      iv. Cash flow
   b. Team
      i. Staffing
      ii. Morale

      iii. Training

      iv. Turnover

   c. Systems/Processes

      i. Human resources

      ii. Operations

      iii. Marketing

   d. Customers

      i. Satisfaction/Loyalty

      ii. Leads

      iii. Referrals

   e. Personal

      i. Hours working

      ii. Family time

      iii. Quality of life

3. Determine where you are today in each of the same above areas.

4. What is the gap between today and where you need to be in 90 days?

5. For each gap, write a SMART goal to close it. Don't worry about the number of goals at this point.

6. Prioritize the goals using the forced matrix in Figure 2.1.

7. For each of the two highest priority goals determine at least two specific tactics for achieving the goal.

8. Then write what steps you and/or your team will take to execute each tactic (see example in Figure 2.2). Be as specific as possible including what will be done, by whom, and the date of completion. Make sure the actions are put in the proper sequence.

9. Create a calendar or timeline (Gantt Chart) that will be posted and/or shared with everyone having responsibility for any defined actions. Create a goals board to visualize what success looks like.

10. Finally, determine how you will reward yourself and your team when the goals are achieved.

The process is pretty straightforward as you can see. One of the keys is to repeat the process every 90 days. While it's important to have longer term goals, I've found that the timelines are too far out to have significant meaning. Every team I have worked with or on did not start focusing seriously on goals until the last quarter of the year. In fact, research shows that the nearer you are to a goal the more you pay attention to it and are motivated to achieve it.[2] That same research also showed that the nearer the goal is to its completion point, the more visualization increases the odds of achieving the goal.

Another way to look at the topic of goal setting is what I call the process of closing the gap. Goals are simply the method by which you close the gap between where you are today and where you want to be. From this perspective, steps 2–5 of the process are the meat and potatoes because that is where you determine the gap and how you will close it.

It is also important to note that determining action steps (step 8) is critical for several reasons. First, action steps determine how you will achieve your goal and define the process for getting there. You cannot go from point A to point B in one fell swoop; there must be interim steps taken. Try going from one end of a room to the other in one giant leap, impossible unless it's a really small room. Second, action steps assign responsibilities and accountabilities. Who will do what and by when? Again biting off small pieces gets you where you need to be just like eating a sandwich. Creating a visual representation of the action steps with a calendar or Gantt chart and posting it publicly provides accountability for each step as well as transparency on progress. Everyone will know exactly where things stand all the time.

Do not skip the final step. Knowing what the reward is at the beginning is a powerful motivator as long as the reward is something that matters. It doesn't matter what you choose as long as it is significant to you and your team. Another small thing I always have people do before going off to achieve their goals is write a letter of congratulations to themselves complete with a self-addressed envelope. When the goals are reached, I send the letter. It's amazing how much impact this has when the individual receives, opens, and reads this letter they wrote to themselves 90 days prior.

Goal setting is a fun and powerful tool for growth when taken seriously and done regularly. As a small business coach, I had the great fortune

---

[2] A. Cheema, and R. Bagchi. March, 2011. "The Effect of Goal Visualization on Goal Pursuit: Implications for Consumers and Managers," *The Journal of Marketing*, pp. 109–123.

to work with clients to help them set and achieve goals for their business every 90 days. I would rent a meeting room, bring them all together the last week of a given quarter and we would have a goal-setting day. There were two reasons I did it this way. First, they had to take themselves out of the business in order to work on it. Second, they enjoyed getting with other business owners to encourage each other and celebrate the wins. There was always a lot of energy in the room.

On goal-setting day, we started with everyone sharing their successes the previous quarter. They would remind everyone of their goals and then share how they achieved them. Oh, I forgot to mention that at the end of each session, everyone stood up and shared the goals they had set. By doing that and knowing they would be sharing their results the next quarter, they were accountable to everyone in the room. Telling a room full of people what you will achieve is a great motivator. No one wants to come back and share that they failed.

So, after the cheering and clapping for each person as they shared their success, we had a motivational period where I would present some material to get the room in the right mood for the work ahead. Sometimes it was a short video clip from a movie. Al Pacino's locker room speech in *Any Given Sunday* was always a good one. If you've never seen it, look it up on YouTube. Then, we got to work and followed the process listed earlier. And again, at the end, everyone shared the goals they set for the quarter. As a coach, this was always fun day because my clients were excited, engaged, and motivated.

While annual and quarterly goal setting are critical elements to success, I don't want to give you the impression that you should only set annual and quarterly goals. Daily, weekly, and monthly goals are just as important. They create the stepping-stones or action steps that help you reach your larger goals. They also make sure you keep your priorities in the right order so you don't get distracted. It is easy to become distracted with urgent matters that don't have anything to do with your priorities. Allowing yourself to give in to those daily distractions means that when you look back at your day you realize you did not accomplish what you planned to accomplish. I believe that time management is really priority or self-management. Time marches on, no matter what we do. It cannot be managed. To use time effectively, we must prioritize our activities and then be disciplined enough to accomplish tasks in order of their priority.

Setting goals that are aligned with your WHY is the next critical step to success. Earl Nightingale who was a popular radio personality in the 1950s and recorded "The Strangest Secret" once said "People with goals succeed because they know where they are going. It's as simple as that." I wholeheartedly agree with Mr. Nightingale and sincerely hope this chapter won you over to our way of thinking when it comes to goals.

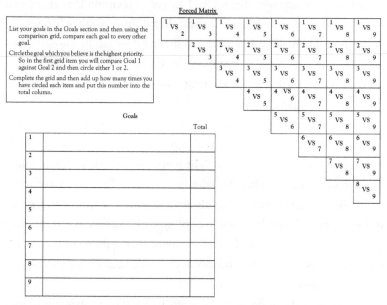

Figure 2.1 Forced matrix

My top goals for the next 90 days are:

Goal #1:	Who	Start Date	End Date
Increase sales by 5% for the quarter compared to the same quarter last year	Team	Jan. 1	Mar. 31
Strategy: Increase leads by 50%	Team	Jan. 1	Jan. 30
Actions:			
Purchase 200 leads from a known reliable source	Me/Owner	Jan. 1	Jan. 7
Create a referral program for previous clients, e-mail it to them and follow	GM	Jan. 2	Jan. 5
Create a Facebook Ad/Post and post it to at least 5 local Facebook groups	Me & GM	Jan. 5	Jan. 8
Strategy: Increase conversion rate from 10% to 15% on qualified leads	Team	Jan. 1	Mar. 31
Actions:			
Create and roll out a 100% satisfaction guarantee	Me/Owner	Jan. 1	Jan. 7
Create incentive if customer buys by a certain date	Me & GM	Jan. 7	Jan. 10
Strategy: Conduct price analysis to determine items that we can	Owner		
Actions:			
Review product line and compare our prices to competitor prices	Owner	Jan. 7	Jan. 14
Determine list of items where we are priced below competition	Owner	Jan. 14	Jan. 21
Determine which of the items where we are below competition we can	Owner	Jan. 21	Jan. 21
Create and issue new price list	Owner	Jan. 22	Jan. 22

Figure 2.2 Goals strategies and action steps

CHAPTER 3

Building a Great Team

To build a successful franchise or other organization: seek out the best people, compensate them the best, share your profits and equity with them, treat them with respect, share your goals and strategies with them, create a family atmosphere, a sense of belonging, and give recognition for accomplishments; make certain your credibility is unquestionable, set the highest possible standards, enthusiastically instill in them your passion to achieve excellence in all your combined endeavors, give the responsibility and authority to achieve, and periodically check and follow through that your standards and philosophies are adhered to.

—Bill Rosenberg

The last two chapters were all about you. Establishing your purpose was all about self-examination and understanding why you got into business. Setting goals is about how you are going to achieve your purpose. Goal setting is also about self-discipline and self-accountability. It is about creating intense focus on achieving an objective. That's all about you.

Unless you bought yourself a job, you will never grow your business without surrounding yourself with great people and building a team. I like to use sports analogies because I think they have great relevance in business so here is the first of probably many you will see in this book. If you think about it, there is not a single successful person in any sport who has done it alone. Even athletes in individual sports such as tennis, golf, swimming, or track have a team around them. They have a coach, a trainer, nutritionists as well as family and friends to support them. Golfers have a caddy who does much more than just carry the clubs. In short, to be successful at anything, you need a team of people who believe in you and your cause.

Some might argue that building a great team is the most important aspect of a successful business. While their argument certainly has merit, I would ask them how they plan to attract the type of people they need without being able to explain where they are going, why they are going there, and what success looks like. The type of people you want around you are people who want to be a part of something and are not just in it for the paycheck.

When I was a young manager running a 24/7 business, I thought hiring people with specific skills and experience was the way to go. I had a lot on my plate and training new people took time and effort. What I learned was that my approach led to high turnover, which took more time than if I simply hired people who cared about customers and had the right attitude and trained them really well. Those people stayed a lot longer and were instrumental in growing the business.

You have likely heard the phrase "attitude is everything" and you probably think it's true. My experience has taught me that it is. To illustrate and communicate this belief to my teams over the years I have used this example. Take the letters in the word attitude and write down its corresponding number in the alphabet like this:

A	T	T	I	T	U	D	E
1	20	20	9	20	21	4	5

When you add up the numbers, the total is 100. Attitude is everything!

What Do Team Members Want?

I'm not a psychologist so I will not go into a deep discussion of the wants and desires of the human race and how all that fits with your responsibility as a leader. I leave that to the professionals. I will, however, use some basic psychology principles in layman's terms to describe generally what people want and why. I'm interested in people and have taken time to pay attention to them, ask questions, and come up with some basic ideas on human nature that I think are universal.

First, there was a psychologist many years ago by the name of Maslow who described a hierarchy of human needs. He used a pyramid to visually describe his hierarchy because each level built on the base formed by the previous levels. Without a strong base, the structure collapses.

At the bottom of this pyramid are basic items all living creatures need to survive such as food, water, warmth, sleep, safety, and security. For humans in the modern world, this means we need money to purchase food, water, and shelter to satisfy our basic needs. Part of this is the ability to live in an area that is reasonably safe from the crimes that challenge our security. Until we do that, our basic needs remain unmet and we continue to seek out ways to meet these needs. For people at the low end of the pay scale in what are commonly known as minimum wage jobs, that's why they will leave a job for 25 cents more per hour. It may not be much but until their basic needs are fully met, any amount will get them closer to the goal.

The next level of needs fall into the psychological category. These are things like love, friends, belonging, and having a sense of accomplishment. Being a contributing member of a team also falls into this realm. It is important to remember that while this level of needs exists even as basic needs remain unmet, their importance only comes to the surface once the first level needs are satisfied. It can be tricky at times to determine which level is driving someone's behavior. For example, you may have a friend making a living more than sufficient to satisfy his level one needs who complains that he's not being paid enough. When you dig a little deeper it turns out he's really leaving because he's not getting acknowledged for exceeding expectations and is using money as a replacement for his level two needs being unmet. If you ever hear someone say, "They're not paying me enough to put up with this nonsense," that's a dead giveaway.

The third and final level of needs are self-fulfillment needs. These include things like reaching your potential and achieving your WHY. Unfortunately, most people will not live a life where these needs come close to being met because the first two levels are not met. This level also requires much more self-awareness and personal responsibility than is required by the other two. By virtue of the fact that you're reading this right now, you deserve congratulations for being part of the minority seeking to fulfill this higher level of human desire.

The point of all this psychological stuff is this, as a leader it is your responsibility to learn about what drives people in general and your people in specific. Then it is your job to provide them what they need to be successful as part of your team. If you want to create a successful company that will allow you to achieve your WHY, it is completely on your shoulders to set the vision that attracts great people and give those people the tools to succeed, which includes creating the environment in which their needs are met and they feel part of something larger than themselves. Think of it this way, your team members are your customers. To you, they must be your number one priority. Take care of them and they will take care of the paying customers who in turn will fuel the success of your business helping you achieve your WHY. It is the business life cycle depicted in Figure 3.1.

The Cycle of Business

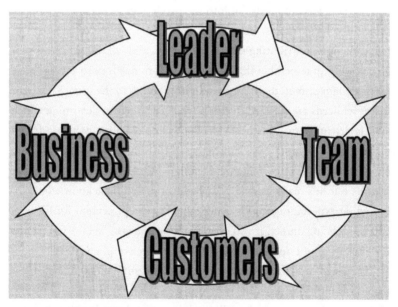

Figure 3.1 Cycle of business

Another way I like to describe this diagram is this:

The experience of your customers will never exceed the experience of your team

If you hire the right people, train and treat them well, they will treat your customers well. The reverse is also true. As the leader of your business, you are ultimately responsible for the performance of your team. You hire them, you train them, you create the culture. The phrase "You can't find good help anymore" is a load of crap. There is not a shortage of good people and never has been. There is a shortage of good leaders. Be a good leader and you will always have good help.

Part of being a great leader is understanding the needs hierarchy and recognizing that you cannot change the laws of nature. People's basic needs must be met first before anything else matters. The challenge is knowing what it takes to meet those basic needs in an ever-changing environment. For example, the debate that has been raging for a number of years is the one around minimum wage. Should there be a minimum wage? If so, what should it be? Is minimum wage meant to provide people a "living" wage or is it more of an entry level kind of thing? My position is that none of that matters. To me it's a supply and demand issue and it involves what I call the "effective minimum wage." Having visited and worked in cities and towns all over the United States has given me exposure to markets where minimum wage is technically $7.25 per hour (the current national rate) and markets in states that have set a much higher minimum rate. No matter what the minimum wage rate is in a market, I have found that what businesses need to pay in order to get people to work for them is always higher than the minimum. That's what I call the effective minimum wage. When the number of applications for a given job decreases, the effective minimum wage increases in an effort to get more applications. That is basic supply and demand.

Carl Casalino is a Long John Silver's (LJS) franchisee in Pennsylvania and a former Taco Bell franchisee in Maryland. Carl also owns two independent restaurants in the Baltimore, MD area called The Rumor Meal and The Rumor Reel. I first met Carl in 2016 when I was working for LJS and I was immediately impressed. Carl is one of those rare leaders who cares deeply about his people and understands that without them, he has no business. When I spoke with Carl about the topics of leadership and having a great team, one of the first things he said to me was "As a franchisee for Long John Silver's and Taco Bell, our whole foundation was to keep great people. That's what enabled us to do everything we did."

But even Carl understands that it all starts with satisfying people's level one needs. To quote him:

> For us, we've been fortunate we've had the same people since we opened. you know me as an operator with Long Johns and our reputation with those restaurants, and then also as a franchisee with Taco Bell. Even now, running these family businesses. The Rumor Meal is going on three and a half years, and The Rumor Reel is going on three and a half weeks. So, and it's funny, because we started off, I think, with seven people the week before we started The Rumor Reel, and I'm at 96 right now. In the last three and a half weeks, we literally hired 90 people, and now the challenge is obviously training everybody getting everybody acclimated to our systems and moving on, but it's gone great. But I could not even get people to walk in the door, especially from a kitchen standpoint, if I wasn't paying somewhere between 15 and 20 bucks an hour. So that's the new foundation for that hourly position. That's what it is. And it was a learning curve for me a little bit. I mean up to this point, we've been able to pay 12 to 15 bucks an hour, you're making 15 you're kind of on the higher end of my kitchen folks. So yeah, it's just different. You got to pay attention to what's happening.

So even for a great leader like Carl, and you will soon see why he is a great leader, paying effective minimum wage is a must if you want to attract good people. If you are not paying at least what your immediate competitor is paying, you're not meeting people's level one needs and you'll struggle with being short staffed.

Hiring the Right People

The next question likely on your mind is where do I find good people? First, remember my definition of good people has little or nothing to do with their skill set. Attitude is everything. I would add passion, energy, and quick to smile to that list. Lynn Given who is a MaidPro franchisee in Parker, CO uses the acronym FAT, which stands for Faithful, Available, and Teachable. When I spoke with Lynn, she described it this way, "First and foremost, attitude. Then: Being Faithful, Available and Teachable (FAT). When an applicant has all of these characteristics, we are able to help them to be successful within our organization." Lynn has built a very successful business over the years and was named a 2021 Rockstar Franchisee by Franchise Business Review.

Lynn also told me she finds most of her people from recruiting sources such as:

1. Online sources like Indeed.com or Snagajob.com;
2. Organic postings such as Facebook postings;
3. Flyers in grocery stores and other retail establishments; and
4. A team member referral program.

There are many other sources you can use but here are some things I would stay away from in today's world:

1. Newspapers are a thing of the past. Even using online classified ads gets little to no response.
2. Help wanted signs on reader boards or in your windows unless you are opening a new location. For an established business this sends a message of desperation to potential team members and signals to your customers that you are understaffed. Not a good message.

Find the sources being used by the people you want to hire and use those. If you are looking to hire people between the ages of 18 and 25, talk with some of them and ask where they're looking for jobs then place your ads there. This is also one of the reasons why a team member referral program is a great source. If you talk with the good people who already work for you, you will find they recommend other good people especially if you give them a bonus once the new person is hired and stays at least 90 days.

Going back to Carl Casalino for a minute, I asked him how he went from seven people a week before opening his new restaurant to 96 people three weeks later. Here is his response:

Well, a couple of things. I was really going after some high end people. I was trying to get a GM. I was trying to get a chef. I was looking for leaders because I thought if I get some really good leaders in here, they're going to get me some people. They've been in the industry a long time and if they're good, usually their people follow them. So I was able to find one guy that was very much like that. He brought me not a chef, the guy was more of a sous chef. Anyway, it was snowballing as far as my kitchen goes, for the front of the house. I wasn't nearly as concerned about that. We're in a community of a very abundant amount of 18- to 25-year-old kids that are either going to college or they're going to trade school or they're doing something locally, and they stay local. So they're looking for a bartender serving shift, a bussing shift, just something to work around their schedule, and those people flooded in once we open the doors. Nobody wanted to come to a closed restaurant, because we couldn't give them answers like when can I start? Well, we're not sure we're waiting on the health department. We're waiting on this. We're waiting on that. And they wanted jobs right now and this is ironically right when schools are letting out so it was May. Kids are coming out of school. They want a summer job. Don't want to hear we're not open until July, right? So that's a little bit what happened. I had some really good kids walk in the door. But I couldn't really keep them because I couldn't promise them when they were going to start. So it was interesting. The timing was probably not the best.

So, Carl's approach with at least part of his team is to find solid, experienced leaders at key positions and they will bring people with them. That is often what happens in large corporations who hire a new leader. That leader brings her or his own people in. If that leader has cultivated a strong culture and team loyalty, he or she will always have people following.

The other difficulty you are likely facing is competition from companies in your area who can afford to pay more than you can pay. I spoke with Cindy Gray who is a ComForCare franchisee in the Orlando, FL area. Cindy said she is not just competing with other agencies like hers, she is also competing with Walmart, Target, and Walgreens who can afford to pay more. I asked Cindy how she competes for people given that level of competition. Her reply was very revealing.

> Most of our employees just come through an application. But once they come in our door, they realize we are very different than our competitors are in this market. I'm a nurse by background and I think they see you and feel right away, a different culture, when you walk in our door, they see that we truly care about them as much as we do our clients. They know that we work hard to try to help them make more money if they can. When you walk in our front door right over right in front of you is a big archway that says we love our caregivers. That's one of the first things they see. And then now more and more of course, we're getting word of mouth, I put out recruiting bonuses $100 recruiting bonus to any caregiver that could send me a caregiver that day and we got one, but it was well worth it. She was awesome.

You may look at that and say great but how do I get people to fill out an application? The answer is you have to get the word out. You need to let people know in your advertising how great you are. In the next chapter, I will talk about creating customers who are raving fans. If you want to attract good people, you need to have team members who are raving fans. Here is how Cindy put it.

> And the caregivers. when I talk to them, they just can't stop saying how much they love working for us, and how different it is to work for our agency than any other agency they've ever worked for before. That we do so much more for them. And they feel like we care about them. And we do and we do a lot. I put a lot of my extra money, I got to a point that for me spending marketing dollars on a billboard or print ad or anything like that was not as valuable as taking that same marketing money and putting it into my caregivers, quality caregivers. Because if you think about it, that is our marketing. When we send the caregivers out into the community and then with clients. They don't represent well; we don't do well.

Imagine spending your marketing budget on taking care of your team. Crazy right? Not really. Instead of renting a static billboard or placing an ad, how about having living, breathing humans be your marketing. Is there anything that will sell your business better than the passion of your team?

Keeping Good People

Of course, the happier your team is, the more likely they are to stay with you and that is the best recruiting method by far. It just makes sense that the more you retain team members, the less you need to recruit new ones. And let's not forget the financial impact on your business. Turnover is expensive. How expensive depends on a multitude of factors and varies by salary level and industry. The bottom line is that when you factor in the cost of recruiting, screening, interviewing, onboarding, and training alone the number is north of $1000. Add in lost productivity while the new team member gets up to speed, and the higher rate of mistakes new people make, the cost increases substantially. Turnover can also negatively impact your top line sales numbers in that customers don't like seeing new faces all the time. Customers like consistency and certainty so when they see new faces, they have less confidence in the experience they will receive. I will discuss this aspect in more depth in the next chapter so for now believe me, team turnover can cost you customers.

There are a few common reasons why businesses experience turnover. Some turnover is unavoidable and out of your control and some is self-inflicted. You can't prevent the first kind but you can plan for it. The second type is completely preventable but requires taking a hard look in the mirror.

Unavoidable turnover includes things such as people moving, going to college, caring for a sick loved one, and retirement. Usually you know about these events ahead of time, although caring for a sick loved one can come about quickly. The point here is that some turnover is inevitable so you always need to be prepared. Sometimes you can cross-train team members so when someone leaves, someone else can step into their position. Sometimes you can maintain part-time team members who can pick up more hours while you hire and train a replacement. Each business will be different but there are usually options to prepare for unavoidable turnover.

The other kind of turnover is much harder to deal with because it takes reflection and being brutally honest with oneself. There is a saying in business that people don't leave jobs, they leave bosses. While there are "bad" bosses out there, that does not always mean that people leave because their boss is a jerk. It does mean that the reasons people leave are within the control of company leadership. In a December 12, 2018 article for SHRM.org, Roy Maurer cited several studies that determined the main reasons people sought a new job or left for another position.[1] As you would expect, many leave for higher pay or better benefits. Others leave for promotion opportunities and career changes. Other top reasons are work/life balance and bad bosses. Interestingly, every one of the top reasons is within the control of company leadership.

Now you can put in place systems to survey people and find out what is important to them so you can have policies in place to provide whatever it is. That gets complicated and can be hard to keep up with. The other option is to simply know your people and hire/develop leaders who genuinely care about their people. If your company culture is one that cares about people, you and your leadership team will automatically want to know your team members on a personal level. Carl Casalino explained it better than I ever could.

> You have to first believe that people are the number one most important thing. So I start off with the premise that, yeah, I'm in this business, I actually really enjoy the people I'm working with. And I look for the people I enjoy. If I don't enjoy working with you, I'm probably not even going to care about all the things you could possibly do for me, right? Because the problem is, it doesn't fit in with my ability to show my heart and to be able to give you what you need to be successful. So, I initially look at myself, as someone who can give someone else an opportunity to do what their talents are. I want to give them whatever they need to be

[1] R. Maurer. December 12, 2018. "Why are Workers Quitting Their Jobs in Record Numbers?," *SHRM.org*.

the best that they can be. My ability to kind of figure out what that is for that person comes because I become extremely friendly with them. I become not invasively friendly, but I know the things I need to know about their personality. What excites them. How do I make them come to work with a smile on their face? And then what is the thing they are really trying to get out of this relationship. It's not all about me. What are they really looking for? And it's very different for different people.

When Carl talked about the things people need to be successful, he wasn't just talking about intangibles like atmosphere, leadership, and caring. He was also talking about tangible skills which are taught and developed through training and ongoing feedback. Training is the first critical piece of not only reducing team turnover, but it is also critical to your company's success. Remember I shared earlier about when I was a young manager in a 24/7 business? Before I learned how to hire the right people, I had a lot of team turnover. Most of my turnover happened in the first three months after a new team member came on board. I was always short-handed and so I would hire people in bunches and give them a crash course on how to do their job. I called that training. I remember once I even trained five new people all at once and then had them work a shift the very next day. They didn't last long and I don't blame them.

Giving people the tools and setting them up for success is essential to you and to them. Customers don't understand when someone is poorly trained and cannot execute their job. They just think the person is stupid or incompetent and the team member feels that way. When I encounter this, I always ask if the team member is new and tell them it's OK. I don't blame them, I blame the leader for not properly protecting his or her team member with proper training.

Don't just take it from me though. Here is what Lynn Given had to say about training her team:

Training is the key to the success of the business. Without well trained staff we have unhappy customers and then it becomes a cycle of uncertainty. We start with 4 days of training in the field and then ongoing training each week in the office with reminders of our policies and techniques. We find that repetition is key. We coach and train on the go daily. Then reward the team and share the joys.

I have told many leaders and business owners over the years that if they are not willing to spend at least 25 percent of each day in some form of training, put the "for sale" sign on the door today because the value of your business will only go down from here. I believe that statement with my entire being. A leader's number one responsibility is to train, coach, and give feedback to his or her team. Everything else comes second.

How to Train Your Team

Training is different than teaching and so requires a different process. Teaching is the transfer of knowledge from one person to the other. Training is the transfer of knowledge and skills, thus the saying those who can, do and those who can't, teach. I might modify that saying to those who can and do, train.

The first thing to know in order to effectively train someone in a new skill is that the more of their five senses you involve, the faster they will acquire the skill. Generally, you will engage their hearing, sight, and touch most of the time. In some cases, you may be able to engage taste and smell but that will depend on the skill you're training. To engage as many senses as possible follow the five-step method:

1. Tell them what they need to do.
2. Show them how to do it.
3. Let them try.
4. Provide feedback, that is praise good results (or near good results) and redirect if needed.
5. Provide practice opportunities with feedback.

Most of this five-step process is intuitive in that you probably read the five steps and said, "that makes sense." If you have children you used this process thousands of times. Anytime you taught them anything you used this process. The key to skill development is feedback, which I will talk about in detail in a moment. First let me go back to what I said earlier about involving the five senses.

Involving your trainee's senses of sight, hearing, and touch are universal no matter what task you are training. You will tell them what to do (hearing), show them (sight), and have them try (touch). Taste and smell can be more challenging depending on the task. In the food business, taste and smell are universal as well. If you are training someone to make food and are not having them taste it and having them notice the proper smells, you need to re-evaluate your training methods. For instance, when I worked at Arby's and was training someone to properly slice roast beef, I taught them that the thickness of the slice made a big difference. I then made a sandwich with the proper thickness and one with the slice too thick and had them taste each one. They immediately tasted the difference and realized that customers would too. Incidentally, the different thicknesses also have a different smell. If you own a cleaning company, don't just train your team what dirty versus clean looks like and feels like, train them what it smells like too.

So, let's talk about feedback. Author Ken Blanchard is credited with coining the phrase "Feedback is the breakfast of champions." I bet you thought it was Wheaties. I agree with Mr. Blanchard that feedback on performance is the key to improving performance and developing a team. Think about it. When a golfer hits a golf ball the feedback is immediate. The golfer adjusts alignment and swing elements based on the result of the last ball he or she hit. Without feedback, there is no point in practicing. Practice without feedback is a waste of time because that old adage that practice makes perfect is incorrect. Perfect practice makes perfect and you only get closer to perfection with feedback.

Feedback is also neither positive nor negative. Feedback is simply the information received as the result of an event or action. When a microphone is too close to the speaker, the sound from the speaker is received into the microphone and causes feedback. If that happens, you know immediately that you need to move the microphone or turn it off. It's similar with people. When a baby is hungry it cries. The baby's mother is not sure what is causing the crying but she knows it's one of only a few things. She may first check the baby's diaper and when she finds that's not the problem, she tries feeding the baby. When the mother's actions cause the baby to stop crying, she knows she found the problem and the solution. Eventually, mom begins to recognize the subtle differences in the baby's cries and knows exactly what the problem is. Just another example of how feedback works to make people better.

Giving your team members feedback on performance is somewhat similar except you are not just trying to stop undesirable behavior. With team members you also want to redirect undesirable behavior to something more productive and more importantly you want to reinforce desirable behavior so that it continues. In other words, focus on catching people doing things right. So, feedback is a tool to reinforce and redirect behavior.

Feedback is also how you develop talent. The three keys to successfully using feedback to develop your team are what you say, when you say it, and how you say it. What I am about to tell you may sound contradictory, so let me explain before you close the book and throw it in the trash. Earlier I said that feedback is neither positive nor negative. When taken on its own that is a true statement. In the context of using feedback as a tool to develop your team though, if feedback is given in the manner that I am about to describe, it is all positive in that it is intended to help that person improve their knowledge and skills so that they are better able to achieve their dreams. So, let's talk about the what, when, and how.

When giving feedback, what you say must be specific and focused on behavior. It must also start with something the team member does well and finish with an opportunity for improvement. Everyone has strengths or things they do well. Everyone also has opportunities for improvement, not weaknesses but opportunities. Calling them opportunities is a more positive way to look at it and people are a lot more receptive to this language than when you use words like weakness. Trust me, I have used both and opportunities works a lot better. Be specific when describing what they are doing well and always start with this. Starting with the good stuff makes people more receptive to exploring ways to improve. And it is always about behavior or results, never about the person.

For example, when I was in the restaurant business, I would do what we call a supervisor's walk with managers and district managers. We would walk around the restaurant looking at cleanliness, building and team appearance, food quality, and so on, and talk about what was good and what opportunities there were to improve. I always made the managers tell me the good stuff first. They were not allowed to give me any opportunities until they gave me at least three good things. I wanted them to realize there were a lot of things going right and not overlook them. Every one of those managers thanked me for approaching things this way. They always said that throughout their career, the only feedback they got was a list of what they needed to fix. I never did that, I made sure I pointed out the good things and then helped them see the opportunities. If they saw that they had opportunities, the list of things to fix was their list not mine. They had ownership and were committed to making the improvements.

I have also had to deliver feedback to team members, which I knew would be difficult for them to hear. It was critical that I laid the groundwork so the team member knew my goal was to help not hurt. Here is how it went.

I was managing a team of field representatives who all worked remotely. Most of my interactions with them were phone calls but periodically I visited them in the field and we traveled their area together. This particular team member was having relationship issues with members of another department based in the home office. The department leader approached me one day and described some of the demanding and confrontational calls her team was having with my team member. She told me her people did not want to talk with my team member and were not wanting to give my team member what she needed to do her job. I took a deep breath and said I would take care of it. I was scheduled to travel with this team member within a couple of weeks and knew this was a face-to-face conversation.

On my next trip, we visited locations the first day and then we had dinner together. During dinner I said I have something I need to discuss and she immediately tensed up. I told her she was a valued member of the team and gave her two or three things I thought she did very well. I said that I viewed a critical piece of my job as helping my team become even better at their jobs and achieve consistently better results over time. I reassured her that the feedback I was about to give her was meant in that spirit. Then I asked her to describe to me her relationship with the other department. She said it was strained and she was unhappy with the lack of cooperation she was getting from them. We then discussed possible reasons for the situation and I asked her if there was anything she might be doing to create or promote the situation. Because the tone of the conversation was one of making things better, she was open to exploring how she was contributing to the situation. I shared the feedback I had gotten from the department manager and we brainstormed ways she could approach her conversations differently. We concluded with an action plan that included her bouncing things off me prior to having tough conversations with the other department. She then thanked me for being honest and kind at the same time. She said no one had ever bothered to talk with her about her opportunities and help her improve. I reassured her that I saw these types of conversations as my most important responsibility as a leader.

About two months later, I was at the home office and the department leader pulled me aside and asked me how I had affected such a dramatic change with my team member. Her team was talking about how different their interactions with her were and how they were beginning to change their approach to working with her. I explained the conversation we had over dinner while traveling, and how we were working together to help my team member grow in this area. The department leader thanked me saying she appreciated me helping improve the situation. I thought to myself, after all those times of fumbling similar situations Dave, you finally got it right.

This lesson in providing effective, growth-oriented feedback is the most valuable lesson I have learned in my career.

Early in my career I thought that there was such a thing as negative feedback. Telling someone what they were doing "wrong" was negative feedback and I was a jerk for doing it. The funny thing is, I still believe this. When all you do is go around correcting people's performance, you are being negative and a jerk. That is not giving feedback. That is called intimidation. Remember the golden rule and treat people as you would like to be treated then take it a step further. Treat people as they would like to be treated with fairness, empathy, and compassion. That also means holding them accountable for what they have agreed to do and how they have agreed to behave. Not holding people accountable is the opposite of being fair with them. You do them no favors by letting them get away with stuff. Just don't be a jerk about it.

So how do you hold people accountable and not be a jerk? By setting goals. Agree on the goal, the reward for achieving it and the consequences for not achieving it. Recall near the end of the last chapter I wrote about setting daily and weekly goals and acting according to the priorities you set. One of the greatest lessons you can give to your team is to teach them how to do the same. In their book "The One Minute Manager,"[2] Ken Blanchard and Spencer Johnson talk about setting One Minute Goals and following them up with One Minute Praises or One Minute Reprimands. The idea is to set short-term goals frequently with your team. When they hit the goal, give them a one-minute praise. When they don't hit it, give them a one-minute reprimand but only if they are experienced at the task. If the goal was something the team member never did before and they did not hit the mark, your response should be to redirect their behavior by reviewing the procedure and having them try again. Blanchard and Johnson are also very clear that when giving One Minute Reprimands, be sure to focus on the behavior and not the person. In fact you finish with a praise by telling him or her how good they are, how this is not their usual high level of performance, and how they are much better than this. Personally, while I am a huge fan of Ken Blanchard and Spencer Johnson and have read all or mostly all of their books, I am not a big fan of the One Minute Reprimand. I believe that if you set up a culture of trust and your people know you are about them and want them to succeed, then you set goals properly and lay out the rewards and consequences, you will not need to reprimand anyone. Your team members will reprimand themselves when they miss the mark. Your role at that point will be to ask a simple question, what did you learn from this? Part of creating a culture of trust is living by the motto that we do not fail, we either win or we learn. When your team misses the mark, make sure they learned from it and then build them up so they are determined to not have a repeat performance. That is leadership!

When I had my coaching business, I had a client who struggled with staying focused for more than a few minutes at a time. He would get distracted by e-mails coming in or just his own thoughts. He needed to

---

[2] K. Blanchard, and S. Johnson. 1982. *The One Minute Manager*. United States: William Morris & Co.

develop some discipline, which I knew would not happen overnight. At one of our first coaching sessions, we discussed ways to improve his focus and set some very short-term goals. We started by having him disable all the e-mail notifications on his laptop, phone, and so on. He also agreed to put his phone on do not disturb while he was working. It was important for us to agree on these two things because I could then get him to agree to let me hold him accountable for them. Next, we agreed that he would set one of those manual egg timers for 15 minutes and he would work without stopping until the timer went off. If he made it the whole 15 minutes, he was then allowed to check e-mail for five minutes as a reward. Every week when we met, we reviewed his progress and gradually increased the timer amount until after a few months he reached the point where he would set the timer for 50 minutes and give himself a 10-minute reward. There were weeks when he would not increase the timer because he did not achieve his goal. Those weeks I reminded him of his commitment and held him to his agreement. I also made sure to remind him that he had made great progress to that point and that I believed he would make it to the finish line. Even though he was gaining confidence he still need encouragement at times. Don't we all?

Years ago, I was a trainer for Dunkin' Donuts at Dunkin' Donuts University or DDU. DDU was the place that all franchisees came to be trained before they opened their shop or when they bought an existing shop. We trained a lot of people during the five years I was there. I was fortunate to work with many smart and experienced people one of whom was a man named Larry. Larry was self-educated beyond high school. He never attended college but was assessed with the knowledge level of someone with a graduate degree. In short, he was a smart man; perhaps the smartest person I have ever known and I learned a lot from him. It was from Larry that I learned about spending at least 25 percent of your day in some sort of training or put the for sale sign on the door. He would say that to every new group of trainees.

What Larry meant was that there is nothing you will do as a business owner that is more important than training and developing your team and if you cannot or will not do that every day, the value of your business will only go down. Everything depends on how much and how well you train and develop people. To be successful you need to either be wired to think that way or you need to hire someone who is.

Developing a team takes time. People are not robots. Sometimes they will surge ahead and then take a step or two back. Other times they will make steady progress for a while and then hit a plateau. It is your job as a leader and their coach to encourage them and make sure they don't get down on themselves. Hold them accountable and reset when needed. Give honest feedback and remind them of their value. Remind them also that you have their back because as a leader that's your job and their success is your success. If you read no other chapter of this book, read and take this one to heart. How you lead and develop a team is the most crucial aspect of success not just in business but in life.

I will leave this topic with this. Someone once asked a speaker during a presentation this question, "What happens if I spend all this time training people and they leave?" The speaker's response was "What happens if you don't train them and they stay?"

CHAPTER 4

Customer Loyalty

Customer satisfaction is worthless. Customer loyalty is priceless.
—Jeffrey Gitomer

It is amazing to me that in 2021 people continue to speak about customer satisfaction as if it should be the objective of every business to have satisfied customers. That may have been true 50 years ago. In my view, it hasn't been true for at least the past 20 years. Satisfied customers are nice but satisfied does not go far enough in today's competitive marketplace. Businesses must strive for customer loyalty. Why? What's the difference?

Satisfied customers like you. They will probably use your services again or visit you again. They are also likely to visit a competitor if given an incentive. The incentive could be a coupon. In the retail business maybe the incentive is your competitor's more convenient location. It doesn't matter what the incentive is, the fact remains that satisfied customers will not go to you exclusively.

Loyal customers by definition are loyal to you and/or your business. You have won them over to the point that they will forsake all others in favor of you. For example, many years ago I began using a dry cleaner to wash and press my business shirts every week. His name is Mahesh and I started using him for two reasons: his prices were good and he was next to my bank. Every Saturday, for years, I would go to the bank and the dry cleaner. In addition to doing a good job with my shirts, Mahesh quickly learned my name and greeted me with a handshake, a "Hello David," and some small talk. I soon learned that Mahesh knew all of his customers by name.

Often, we talked about golf as he learned early on that we both enjoyed playing and watching the professionals. At some point, we began playing golf together from time to time. We became friends.

One day, a salesperson from a new dry cleaner rang my doorbell. He offered not only better prices than Mahesh but also free pickup and delivery. How could I possibly say no? Well, I did say no. There was simply no way I could betray my friend Mahesh even for lower prices and more convenience. That is the difference between being a satisfied customer and being loyal.

There is a concept common in customer service training called the "Loyalty Ladder." I suspect it was created by management guru Ken Blanchard as the goal of the ladder is to create what Blanchard called "Raving Fans." The concept is simple and illustrated in Figure 4.1:

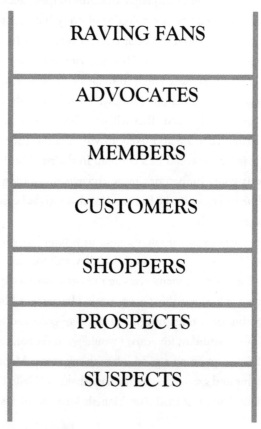

Figure 4.1 Loyalty ladder

As when climbing any ladder, you start on the bottom rung. Here, we find your Suspects. These are people in your target market. They meet the geographic and demographic criteria for your business.

On rung number two are Prospects. Prospects have made themselves known to you in some way so that you can collect their contact data. They may have responded to an online ad asking about your product or service.

Next are Shoppers. These folks have made a purchase from you but are not sure they will make a second purchase.

Customers are people who have purchased from you more than once and likely will again. They may also purchase from your competitors.

Members have downloaded your app and are receiving regular communication and rewards from you.

Advocates are members who give you testimonials and refer new business to you. These are the people who write you five star online reviews and when a friend asks, they refer your company.

The highest rung on the ladder are Raving Fans. These wonderful people don't wait to be asked; they go out and tell everyone they know and meet about your business. In effect, they become your marketing department.

You're probably thinking right now, "That's all good stuff, but how do I get people to be Raving Fans?" Excellent question. The answer is simple, do all the things you are reading about in this book!

Seriously, the concept is simple to understand and difficult to achieve. You need to create a personal relationship with everyone who uses your product or service. And when I say you, I mean you and everyone on your team. More than that, you need to create a positive emotional response. The difference between an advocate and a raving fan is emotion. Advocates like you and will speak well of you when prompted. Raving fans love you and will sing your praises without prompting.

So how do you create a personal relationship with all these people? The same way you have created every other personal relationship in your life. Learn about them. Take a personal interest in them. Ask questions about family, likes and dislikes. Cultivate a friendship over time and teach your team how to do the same. Be like Mahesh. Show them you care about them and they will care about you in return.

Creating a personal relationship is also about understanding the individual needs of each customer and providing them every time. If you own a massage center, keep a profile on each customer with their preferences for music, light levels, and so on, and have the room set ahead of time. It often does not take much to make a customer feel different from every other customer. It does however create an experience that can create a raving fan.

Everything in the previous chapter applies here and must happen before you can even think about building a loyal customer base. Someone very wise once said, "The experience of the customer will never exceed the experience of the team member." I believe many people have said that. I have no idea who said it first. Remember Cindy Gray from ComForCare? I also spoke with Cindy about how she created a loyal customer base. One of the things she said to me was:

> Well, first is caregivers to clients. If your caregivers, your employees are not happy, and you're sending them into your clients' homes, they talk. And, you know, as much as we try to teach them what's appropriate and not appropriate, they say what they want to say that they're not happy. They're going to tell the clients that it's not a good work environment.

It goes back to what Cindy said about having a great team. If you do not make raving fans of your team members, you will never make raving fans of your customers. The experience of the customer will never exceed the experience of the team member! And the benefits are there. As Cindy put it:

> I got to a point that for me spending marketing dollars on a billboard or print ad or anything like that was not as valuable as taking that same marketing money and putting it into my caregivers. Quality caregivers. Because if you think about it, that is our marketing. When we send the caregivers out into the community and then with clients. They don't represent well. We don't do well.

As with everything else in YOUR business, customer loyalty begins with YOU, the owner. If you do not walk the walk, your team won't either. Remember what Henry David Thoreau said, "What you do speaks so loud that I cannot hear what you say." In other words, actions speak louder than words. And you are not allowed to have a bad day when it comes to your customer experience. It doesn't matter what else is happening in your life. As the leader, you are front and center every day.

One thing I learned through the years is that the first thing customers want is a consistent experience. In fact, consistency is so critical that even an average experience every single time is better than average one day and excellent the next. We all have a lot going on in our lives and have a lot on our minds. The last thing any of us wants or needs is to wonder if our experience with a business will be good or bad today. It simply is not worth the risk. We would rather go to a business where we know the experience may not be great but it also won't be bad. We don't need the added stress in our lives.

Consistency starts with keeping team turnover to a minimum. How can you create a consistent customer experience if you are constantly turning over team members? For example, when I was operating a Dunkin', I learned that my customers hated seeing new faces behind the counter all the time. To a customer, a new face means inexperience, mistakes, and slow service. It adds doubt into their experience and doubt erodes trust. And it's even worse with regular customers.

Regulars are the heart and soul of any business. They are the 20 percent of your customers who give you 80 percent of your business. Going back to my Dunkin' days, they were the ones who we saw coming, knew where they were going to sit, and had their order on the counter as they sat down. In your business, they are the customers who might call at the last minute to change their order or ask for their home to be cleaned on Thursday this week instead of Friday and you accommodate them with pleasure. The goal is for every customer to be a regular and the way that happens is to treat them like a regular, whether they are or not.

Of course, you always want to improve the experiences your customers receive in your business; you just need to make sure it happens a little at a time. It is better to make a one percent improvement each week for a year, than it is to improve by 52 percent all at once. Small, incremental improvements can be maintained and become part of your standard operating procedures over time. Large, sudden improvements cannot be maintained and that is where the inconsistency comes in. Athletes train to build up muscle gradually over time, which also builds stamina and endurance. You must build your customer experience the same way.

You may have noticed that I use the term "customer experience" rather than customer service. I do that because creating raving fans is about the entire experience customers have with your business. We can all relate to this because we are all customers. How you feel about a business is determined by the breadth of experiences you have with that business over time. Customer feelings are the ultimate judge because we are all emotional beings and we act based on our feelings. As much as we may want to be Mr. Spock and act solely based on logic, we are not Mr. Spock.

So, if you do not know the three or five things that will drive your customer's good feeling about your business, figure them out quickly and figure out how to satisfy them.

If your franchisor uses a customer feedback tool of some kind, embrace it and use it to create raving fans. If your franchisor does not have a tool that gives you customer feedback, tell them to get one and go find one you can use in the meantime. Customer feedback is important but only if you act on the information. There are a lot of tools out there beyond Google or Yahoo reviews. We've all seen them on our receipts offering something free or a chance to win something in exchange for our feedback. These tools give you a lot of information that can pinpoint opportunities for you to improve and to reward your team.

In some industries, it may be easier to get customer feedback on individual team members. You may assign team members to specific clients or accounts, so you can speak directly to those customers and get direct feedback. In retail-based businesses such as food, oil change, or hair care, it can be more difficult. The beauty of a survey-based customer feedback tool is that it allows you to see trends by day of the week, time of day, type of visit, and so on. You can then figure out if you, for example, have staffing or training opportunities at specific times. I have been able to help franchisees in several brands recognize opportunities to improve customer experience on certain shifts such as Friday evening or Sunday lunch, just by looking at the data with them and combining that with other information like how many people were scheduled, what was their experience level, and who was leading the shift. With all of that, we were able to create action plans for hiring, training, and development to improve the customer experience.

For multiunit franchisees who cannot be in every location every day, this type of information is invaluable. In one case, I was working with a Long John Silver's franchisee who had just over 20 locations. As you would expect, some locations did better with the customer experience than others. As I mentioned previously, one of the reasons for this is the focus on training and team member development in each location. When we dug into the data, it was interesting what we learned.

Four of this franchisee's locations performed significantly above the rest of his locations when it came to customer experience scores. They were clearly doing something the others were not. As it turns out, these four locations were using the brand training programs at a much higher rate than all the others. Because Long John Silver's had a computer-based training program, we were able to look at the number of team members at each location who had completed the appropriate training modules for their position. This showed up on a report as the training completion percentage for the location. What we found was that the four locations with higher customer experience scores also had significantly higher training completion percentages. When I say significant, I mean more than 20 percent higher in every case. The numbers clearly illustrated what we already knew; trained team members provide a better customer experience than untrained team members. This said nothing about the quality of training or the number of training hours; it was much more basic than that. Simply hold managers accountable to using the tools provided and you will have happier customers.

Fortunately, this story has a happy ending. At a regular meeting of all his general managers, the franchisee allowed me to present this information. The four managers of the high performing locations were recognized and rewarded and asked to talk about how they execute training. They shared their best practices and answered questions from the rest of the team. We then challenged everyone to make sure every team member completed all the training for their position over the next 30 days. To their credit, they came very close. They achieved a 97 percent completion rate overall in 30 days (100 percent took a little longer but they got there). The other thing that happened was their customer experience scores started going up. Over a 90-day period, they saw an increase of four to five points depending on the location and as a result of the happier customers, sales also increased. All that from just making sure team members watched some videos and answered some questions. This organization still has much work ahead on their journey to creating raving fans, but this experience was a good first step for them. They learned some valuable lessons, not the least of which is one I mentioned earlier that bears repeating:

The experience of the customer will never exceed the experience of the team

Creating a loyal fan base in your business is exactly like owning a sports team. Filling the stadium every game requires a talented team that is well trained, well coached, and has a strong desire to win. It also takes a leader who can keep them focused on performing at a consistently high level every play while minimizing mistakes. If everyone in the organization works together toward the goal of creating a loyal, raving fan base, the seats will be filled every game. If not, there will be a lot of empty seats or worse, seats filled by the opponent.

I have written a lot about retail-type businesses and business to consumer (B2C) businesses mainly because that is where my experience lies. In the business to business (B2B) world, customer loyalty is more critical because a B2B business typically does not have as many customers and the opportunity to create a relationship is more pronounced. Because there are fewer customers, losing one can devastate the business; so, knowing what each of them is thinking and making them raving fans is paramount.

A tool that seems most effective in a B2B situation is a Net Promoter Score or NPS. It can be a very simple yet very powerful tool. Customers are asked to rate how happy they are with their experience on a scale of 1 to 10. A rating of 9 or 10 is called a promoter. These customers are loyal to your business because of their experiences and will promote or recommend you to colleagues. A rating of 7 or 8 is neutral. You may think these are good scores but these customers would abandon you for a better deal in a heartbeat. A score of 6 or less is a detractor. Not only would these customers abandon you, they are actively seeking a business to replace you and will happily share their poor experiences with others. To calculate your NPS score, take your average promoter score times 10 and subtract your average detractor score times 10. If your average promoter score is 9.5, it becomes 95. If your average detractor score is 5, it becomes 50. Subtract and you have an NPS of 45.

NPS was created by Bain & Company and they remain the gold standard for information on the concept. What I initially found surprising is that on a scale of 1 to 10, a rating of 7 or 8 was not good. Customers who rate you a 7 or 8 are satisfied but not loyal. They are the customers who like you but who will change dry cleaners for a better price and more convenience. They may not be actively seeking your replacement, but will jump ship as soon as something better comes along. If history has proven one truism it's that something better will always come along eventually.

Customers who rate you a 9 or 10 are loyal to you and actively tell others how good you are. They are your raving fans. They benefit your business in several ways.[1]

- **Higher retention rates**—Promoters stay longer and so over their lifetime buy more than other customers. They have what is called a higher lifetime value.
- **Less price sensitive**—They are willing to pay more and are not going to jump ship when you raise your prices (within reason).
- **They spend more**—They upgrade to premium products and services at a higher rate than other customers.
- **More cost efficient**—Because they complain less and pay on time at a higher rate, promoters cost less to service. Also, they refer people to you, which lowers your marketing costs and shortens the sales process both of which save you money.

Once you know your score understanding what it means and how to improve it is key. If you ask people for feedback, you must be willing to act on it. Doing nothing with the feedback you receive is worse than not asking for it in the first place.

You can benchmark your NPS against competitors or other companies in general. A quick Google search for companies with the highest NPS scores will yield you several websites and reports that will give you that information. Frankly, I don't think any of that matters except if you are willing to analyze and implement their best practices. That is a productive effort that will allow you to continuously improve your results no matter what your starting point is.

---

[1] R. Markey and F. Reichheld. March 23, 2012. www.bain.com/insights/the-economics-of-loyalty

Mark Fonseca is the CEO of Primetrix, a company that conducts impartial, third-party surveys for businesses. Mark is an expert in how to conduct and analyze NPS scores and implement changes based on customer feedback. Mark was kind enough to speak with me on the topic and had several insights. Near the beginning of our conversation, I asked Mark why more companies do not use NPS or something similar to understand exactly how their customers view them. It seemed to me that everyone who owns or runs a business would want this kind of information, but sadly that is not the case. Mark told me:

> There's a variety of reasons that they don't do it. It's pride, sometimes they have their head in the sand. They don't know what they don't know and no one's ever really presented it to them. And again, they just might not know about it. You know, ignorance is bliss.

He also said, "You've got the big companies like Chick-fil-A and Apple and the larger companies that know about NPS, but once you get down to $50 million companies and less, not a lot of people know about NPS."

Mark also told me that the process takes a lot of work. Any meaningful changes based on customer feedback require cultural changes in the company and that has to come from the top. Changes are hard. As Mark put it, "Tony Robbins always says, we change for two reasons, pain or pleasure. Either there's enough pleasure or there's enough pain to change." If a company is making money, there is often not enough pain to cause change and it is rarely obvious how much pleasure in the form of additional profit or some other reward will be at the end of the long, arduous road to motivate change.

The rewards for obtaining and acting on customer feedback can be enormous. The four benefits I mentioned earlier are not theoretical. They are real. Mark told me a story that illustrates the point.

> One example is Mike. He did hydraulic hose repair. And he got really good scores, a lot of 9s and 10s. And so I asked the magic question, what could he do to get to an 11, or 12. And a lot of

those customers said, well, while he's in there, fixing the hose, if he could change the air filter, the oil filter, the water filter, and the gas filter, that would help us a lot. And so 17, out of the 30 clients said that would be a great idea. So based on that feedback, he started carrying filters on his vans. And that did two things. It increased his revenue by 12 percent and it locked out his competitors because his competitors didn't do that.

And it doesn't stop there. Here is Mark again. "So Costco is a great example. If you read their internal documents, it says they will not do any advertising. They will grow their business all organically by word of mouth through giving a great customer experience." Costco has some of the highest NPS score of any company in any industry.

Like many things in life, creating raving fans or loyal customers is not complicated and it is also not easy. It requires asking the right questions, listening to the responses, and changing based on what you learn. Change is hard and usually requires a catastrophic event to happen. How many people do you know who did not change their eating or exercise habits until they had a major health crisis? Don't wait for your business to be on life support. You have customers who love you, are indifferent about you, and who will avoid you. Find out why in all three cases and act on what you learn. I promise, you will be happy you did.

CHAPTER 5

Local Marketing

A brand is not just a logo, it's the overall impression and experience you give to your customers.

—Amy Locurto

An operator with whom I worked had a location in a very small and very dead town. When I say dead, I mean that even Walmart moved to a better location. He had an excellent team running the location, it was well maintained and positioned on the main street through town and yet it was down 7 percent versus the previous year and had been down that year too. There was only one thing to do; reconnect with the local community.

Normally when I say local community, I mean the local organizations such as the Chamber of Commerce, the churches, schools, The Rotary, The Elks, and so on. This operator got even more local and literally pounded the pavement for one mile in each direction from his store. He walked into every small business within a mile of his store and spoke with the people in those businesses; those who worked there as well as the customers. He asked how long it had been since they visited his store and asked what was keeping them from visiting. He learned that for the most part his team was doing a good job even though there were a few instances when the product or service were not the best. He learned mainly that people could simply not afford to visit him because times were hard in the town. He then handed them coupons for free food. No purchase needed just come have lunch on us. He also gave them his e-mail and phone number. He asked that they e-mail him about their visit and let them know how it went and if it was really bad, please call him right away and he would fix it. He did this one hour a day until he had visited every business within a mile in each direction. After the first few days, he brought his store manager so he could introduce her to everyone.

He got a lot of e-mails with a lot of feedback. Most expressed thanks for the great lunch and told him they had a wonderful experience. Some gave him feedback on things they could improve. He received no phone calls.

The really cool thing that happened was people would come in and say hello to the manager and call her by name. She did the same as she learned their names. People would see the manager in the grocery store and say hello or chat for a minute. While she did not own the store, she started thinking of it as hers and she went from being a very good manager to being an excellent manager. Every customer was greeted as they entered the store, no exaggeration, every customer! She created a lot of raving fans. And she continued to go out and visit her neighbors periodically and bring coupons. These coupons were for discounts instead of free food but they still were appreciated.

The results of all this activity were remarkable. In the first month, sales went from being 7 percent behind the previous year to 9 percent ahead. That's a 16 percent swing. How is that possible with all the people coming in for a free lunch? Simple, most people feel weird coming in just for free food without buying something. Some would buy a dessert or an appetizer. Others would bring a family member and get two for the price of one. A few came in just for the free food but most bought something. Over time, the results leveled off some as you would expect but through these efforts this store was transformed from just another restaurant slowly dying in a dying town to a vibrant member of the community. The operator and store team demonstrated to the rest of the town that by supporting each other they could get through tough times.

As a franchisee you are likely contributing to a national advertising fund. You may also contribute to a local fund or be part of an advertising co-op. There are many varied ways franchisors collect funds to advertise the brand, all of which can be good if used effectively. Regardless of what your franchise agreement requires you to contribute or spend on marketing, remember the adage that all marketing is local. What that means is to be effective in generating sales, marketing must connect with customers in a personal way.

Traditional advertising methods like TV, while still effective for some things, have become less effective over the past 20 or so years. Even ads on websites and social media sites are becoming less effective. Marketing is becoming more targeted. It is now necessary to create a one-to-one relationship with customers, which must be done on a local level. I didn't really understand this until I became a franchisee.

Paul Reiser and his family owned 38 Sonic Drive In Restaurants until they sold them in the summer of 2021. I had the privilege of speaking with Paul on a number of topics, one of which was local marketing. Even as an owner of 38 locations his family always believed that each location must own its local market. Paul told me this:

> Our average unit volume has always been about 30 percent higher than the national average, even though the size of most of our towns is like three to five thousand people. So we've got these little towns doing two or three million in sales, when the average unit volume for a Sonic is what used to be 1.1 million. So our philosophy has always been just own your local market. What we've really done is owned our neighborhoods, we own the churches, the schools, the chamber commerce in our little towns.

Own your neighborhoods. Own the schools. Own the churches. What does any of that mean? As you might think, it means freezing out your competition as much as possible. It means being the first people there to help when there is a need. I met a Servpro franchisee recently who is on the scene of every house fire in his territory with a kit of essential items for the family like toiletries, stuffed animals for the kids, and similar items. When a family is going through a trauma like losing everything in a fire, bringing them some necessities may seem like a small gesture to you but to them it means much more. How often have you heard about a local Chick-fil-A franchisee bringing water and food to first responders during natural disasters? Yes, they do it because it is the right thing to do. They also know that local people see and remember. Own your neighborhood.

Owning the churches and schools is the same. Participate with more than your pocketbook. Give your time. When the church is sponsoring a food drive, be part of it and have your team be part of it. Many companies offer team members two volunteer days a year with pay. Do you? What if you organized volunteer days and your team showed up for a food drive wearing a logo t-shirt? Several franchisees I know provide coupons to local schools to use as rewards for the kids. Usually it's a free meal or something similar. To me that's known as a no brainer.

Working for national brands, I knew some local marketing was important. I knew, for example, that connecting with schools by buying an ad in the high school paper or advertising on the outfield fence of the baseball stadium were good ways to promote locally. I also knew that elementary schools reward kids for good grades and perfect attendance with coupons for their favorite restaurant, so participating in those programs was important. What I did not realize is that taking an active role in the community by not only being a member of the Chamber of Commerce but being on committees is also important. I also never realized the value of networking.

For some businesses networking has more value than for others and for some, it is a key method for building your business. For a brick-and-mortar retail business like a restaurant, networking is important but not as critical to building sales as for a massage studio or a service business such as senior care, cleaning, lawn care, and so on. Being part of a networking group designed to pass referrals between members has long been the way independent business owners have grown their business. I have not met a lot of franchisees in the networking groups I joined or visited and frankly that surprises me. Yes, networking is time consuming and yes you will need to refer business to your fellow group members. You will also get referrals and build your local reputation faster and more effectively than any other marketing tactic. If you are in the home or personal services industry and are not a member of BNI, Am Spirit, or some other local networking referral group, start visiting some and find one where you feel comfortable and join today.

Service organizations such as Rotary, Kiwanis, and Lions Club are also excellent for networking and building a positive local reputation. These organizations offer loads of opportunity to serve the community and participate in local events. Your team will love this too. In general, people want to be part of something bigger than themselves. They want to contribute to the greater good but don't always know how. They need your leadership to show them and help them.

For a long time, Arby's was a national partner with Big Brothers Big Sisters. Through this partnership franchisees had the ability to support their local chapters by sponsoring events and fundraisers. The franchisee in Dayton, OH, was one of those who embraced the chance to participate. Every year, he sponsored a golf tournament that raised tens of thousands of dollars for the charity. His team loved being part of the day. Many of them prepared and served sandwiches, drove drink carts, or helped determine prize winners for longest drive and closest to the pin. Everyone had a lot of fun on the day of the event but the real fun was had in each of the Arby's locations leading up to the event. For weeks prior, every store collected donations from customers and had fun decorating the walls with the paper hearts representing each donation. It was a competition to see which store could cover the most area. Mainly it gave the teams a sense of pride and accomplishment knowing they were helping the boys and girls in their town. We may not have been able to measure the impact on sales but we knew Arby's in Dayton, OH, had a reputation for helping the community and that always has a positive impact on sales.

Speaking of measuring success, another key element to any local marketing is to have a way to measure its success rate. So if you do a direct mail piece, with a coupon, make sure there is a code on it. If you mail to several zip codes, use a separate code for each. If you have multiple coupons with multiple products or offers, each one has a different code. You have to be able to measure what works and what doesn't so you can keep doing what works and stop what doesn't. Internet advertising and social media work the same way. Every website on which you advertise has its own code. If you are advertising in Facebook groups, each group has a unique code. How else will you know which groups work? This may sound like the proverbial no-brainer, but just the other day I was talking with a friend who has a client who did not know this. Don't feel bad if you didn't either. You don't know what you don't know until you know it, you know?

There are all sorts of research and data available to tell us that traditional forms of mass advertising have been in decline for many years. A quick Internet search will reveal several sources that say television viewership has dropped since sometime in the early 2000s. The proliferation of cable TV channels and streaming services has certainly diluted viewership of specific channels and individual shows. Radio too shows evidence of lower effectiveness as more and more people download the songs they like and listen to what's in their music library. The advent of subscription music services that allow you to listen ad-free is another factor. The way I see it, people continue to seek ways to enjoy the content they like without interruption from annoying ads.

Marketing continues to evolve to find more ways to connect with people on an individual level. Digital marketing records the things for which you search and sites you visit and tailors advertising accordingly. Brands have loyalty apps that allow you to opt into text messages and give you discounts based on past purchases. Even grocery stores send you coupons for things you have purchased in the past. The trends in marketing are to create a personal relationship with the customer without physically interacting with them. It is becoming a 21st-century version of the time when the only nonlocal way to buy something was through the Sears catalog.

In a way these marketing trends are good for franchisees because they level the playing field between small businesses and big corporations. As an individual franchisee aka small business owner, you have the ability to target your customers in your local market either as a group or individually through loyalty apps, social media sites, and text message marketing. The beauty of these methods is that as you follow the process of creating raving fans discussed in the last chapter, you can send relevant marketing to your fans who welcome and embrace it rather than find it annoying.

In its simplest terms, local marketing is really just relationship marketing. It is all about finding ways to create a personal relationship with people in your local area. I don't want to diminish one of the main reasons you likely decided to open a franchised business rather than an independent and that is the power of a brand. There is a lot to be said about being part of a powerful brand that can bring people to you just because of the name. It is one of the reasons I am such a fan of franchising. Relying only on the power of your brand though is a mistake. You have to connect with people on a local level to maximize the potential of your business. If you've joined a brand that understands this you will have tools on which to draw. If you have not, you'll need to create the tools yourself.

In today's world, brands that do not have an app that customers can download on their smart phone is a huge mistake. There are several functions an app will serve, which can vary by the type of business you have. Some let you find the nearest location, give you some industry-related information, and that's about it. Others allow you to order and pay for products, choose pickup or delivery, save your favorite location, and leave feedback or rate the experience. To me that's a full service app.

During the COVID-19 pandemic of 2020, brands that did not have an app scrambled to create one quickly. They realized an app was critical to survival and that they had been slow to adapt to the technology. They learned a valuable lesson. Some brands remained slow to adapt and their franchisees found their own solution. I worked for one of those brands. When the pandemic hit and food businesses had to shift to an order ahead with delivery model, the ones without the ability to do so really suffered. One of the franchisees of the brand I worked for found a third-party app called Chow Now, which allowed customers to order and pay for their food and have it delivered using one of the third-party delivery companies. As we spread the word among the franchisee community and franchisees began signing up, they were able to generate sales instead of shutting down completely. I doubt any of them would have survived without making this shift. As the pandemic eased, and dining rooms began reopening, business started booming. Now, on top of their usual customers physically visiting the locations, they still had a lot of new digital customers continuing to order. As long as you are not violating your franchise agreement and keeping your franchisor informed about your local marketing activities, you should remain open to trying methods that have a good chance of building your business. Remember to set up ways to measure success or you'll just be wasting your money.

One last thing about local marketing and especially networking. It is absolutely best to do the networking yourself. You should join and attend the networking group meetings. You join and be part of the Chamber. I understand though that not everyone is comfortable in those situations. It can be hard meeting new people and putting yourself out there, especially if you are a more reserved personality type. Force yourself to do it and become good at it. No one ever grew by staying in their comfort zone. You will be better for it and so will your business. If you must, find someone to go with you at first and have a feedback session with them afterward. This is your business and you have to do whatever it takes to make it work. Once you build you can integrate your team members into the process as an extension of yourself but never take yourself out of it completely. You are the owner and there is no substitute for you.

CHAPTER 6

Making Money—Know Your Numbers

Profits are better than wages. Wages make you a living; profits make you a fortune.

—Jim Rohn

If you are a first time or new business owner you may read the quote from Jim Rohn above and think "Boy I sure hope he's right." If you are an experienced business owner you might read that quote and your thoughts could go either way. You may think Mr. Rohn was right or you might think he was crazy depending on your experience. I can tell you without question based on the numerous examples of successful business owners that Jim Rohn was absolutely right when he made that statement. No one ever got rich from wages alone. Even the CEOs of big corporations earn most of their money from bonuses and stock options, not salaries. Profits are where it's at.

Profits are also the by-product of everything else you do in your business. There is a reason the profit line on your profit and loss (P&L) statement is called the bottom line. It is called that because it is the end result of every other action, number, and result in your business. The decisions made when determining your purpose, setting goals, building your team, building sales through customer loyalty and local marketing, and every other aspect of your business determine profits. That's why I have and will continue to espouse the notion that if you focus on making good decisions in all the key areas of your business, profits will come. Don't focus on making money. Focus on doing the right things right.

Beyond all that, the key to making money is as the chapter title suggests, knowing your numbers. Every business has key numbers that must be tracked and evaluated. As the owner, you absolutely must know what those numbers are and must know them like you know your name. It was always shocking to me when I asked a franchisee how sales were last week and they didn't know. If business ownership was a college class, knowing last week's sales and how they compared to the same week last year and two years ago would be right at the beginning of the course.

Breakeven Point and Proforma

Before you signed your franchise agreement your franchisor likely required you to submit a break even and cash flow proforma. I hope that was the case because if it was not, I question the competency of your franchisor. Both these documents answer the question of how much sales you need to be profitable. Let's start with the breakeven point or BEP.

As the name suggests, the BEP tells you the sales you need to cover all your expenses or break even. You don't make money and you don't lose money. I will explain why you need to know this number and how to use it shortly. First, let me cover how to calculate it.

Every business has variable costs and fixed costs. Variable costs vary with the amount of sales, so they are expressed as a percentage of sales rather than a dollar amount. The dollar amount will vary but the percentage should not. Hourly labor is a typical variable cost. As your sales increase you will add more labor hours and thus more dollars, but the ratio of labor dollars to sales should remain pretty constant. If not, something is out of whack. More on this later. Other variable costs in your franchise business are royalties and marketing contributions as they are also a percentage of sales.

Fixed costs are the ones that don't change no matter what your sales are. Rent, utilities, loan payments, and salaried labor are typical fixed costs. You may or may not have control over these costs; that is another matter. The point here is that these costs do not vary up or down based on sales.

So, your BEP then is the amount of sales you need to cover your fixed costs after your variable costs are covered. Think of it like a dollar bill. If 40 percent (or 40 cents) of every dollar of sales goes to cover variable costs, that leaves 60 percent (or 60 cents) left to cover fixed costs. The BEP tells you how many times 60 cents needs to come into your business to cover fixed costs. For example, let's say you have $15,000 in fixed costs every month and your variable costs are 40 percent. Divide $15,000 by 60 percent (or 0.60) and your BEP is $25,000 per month. Break that down to a weekly number and it is about $6,250 per week. That's a little bit off because months are not exactly four weeks long but you get the idea.

If you calculated a BEP before you opened your business, it was based on a lot of projections with a few known items such as rent and debt. Now that you are open, you need to recalculate your BEP based on actual numbers. Each time you have a significant change in a cost category like you hire another salaried person due to growth, recalculate your BEP.

Now why is it important to know your weekly BEP? If you know your weekly BEP and you track sales every day, which you should, you know what day of the week you reach breakeven. When you know that, you know what day of the week you start making money. If it takes you seven days to reach breakeven that is an obvious problem. Reduce costs or go out and get more sales quickly. The earlier in the week you reach breakeven, the sooner you begin making money and breathing a little easier. It's also important because once you reach breakeven, for every dollar above it, subtract variable costs and the balance goes straight to the bottom line. We call that flow thru. If variable costs are 45 percent, then for every dollar above breakeven, 55 cents flows thru to the bottom line.

A proforma is simply a projection of what you think your P&L statement will look like for some period of time. You had to include a proforma in your business plan to get financing for your business. As an operating document it is essentially your budget. Comparing your actual P&L to your projected P&L tells you if you are ahead or behind budget and you can take action accordingly. If you are managing a team and paying bonuses based on performance, those bonuses are likely based on actual versus budget results.

Generating Sales

Sales or as I sometimes refer to them, top line, are the lifeblood of business. Without sales you go broke quickly and never realize your WHY. Sales are generated in several ways:

- Marketing/Sales Process
- Brand Name Recognition
- Building a Loyalty Customer Base
- Pricing
- Shifting Business Mix

I may be leaving out a few but these are the methods that will generate the majority of sales for most businesses. Let's start with Marketing.

Marketing/Sales Process

I wrote a lot about local marketing in the last chapter and will not repeat myself. If, however, your business uses salespeople and depends on a process to close deals, that is part of Marketing. As I stated previously, the purpose of Marketing is to generate leads. Turning those leads into customers requires a multiple step process called Sales. Your franchisor likely has a sales process that was taught in your initial training. My advice here is simple. Follow the process!

If you are not hitting your sales projections, it's time to do some analysis to determine where the process is breaking down and why. There really is only one key metric in the sales process and it is your conversion rate. What percent of leads are converted to sales calls, conversations, or estimates? Not every lead will have an interest or need for your product or service so your conversion rate will not be 100 percent. However, if your lead generation (Marketing) is targeting the right list of prospects, you should have a pretty high conversion rate at this point. Your next conversion rate is the percent of prospects who become customers. This conversion rate can and should be very high if you provide a good value and build trust with your prospects. You should be tracking this conversion rate at least monthly and if you have multiple salespeople, know each one's conversion rate. Your franchisor should also be able to tell you what the average conversion rate is for other franchisees. If not, call several franchisees and ask them. If you find your conversion rate slipping or below average, there are many things you can do to improve it. Here is a list of 60 proven ways to increase your conversion rate.

1. Written Guarantee
2. Define Your Uniqueness
3. Provide Quality Products
4. Print a Benefits List
5. Use a Testimonial List
6. Before & After Photos/Demos
7. Show Samples/Example Photos
8. Quality Brochures
9. Information Sheets/Booklets
10. Added Value Offers
11. Product/Price Listings
12. Team Member Profiles
13. Write Company's Magic Story
14. Display Awards/Certificates
15. Allow Mail Order, Home Delivery
16. Point of Sale Displays
17. Use Payment Plans & Financing
18. Daily/Weekly Cost Breakdown
19. Flowchart Your Sales Process
20. Audio, Video Sales Demos
21. Reprint Press Articles
22. Re-write Quotes, Tenders and Proposals Into Action Plans
23. Print Company's Vision/Mission
24. Try Before You Buy
25. In-store Merchandising
26. Sales Scripts
27. Greet Prospects & Use Their Name
28. Introduce Yourself
29. Smile, Build Trust & Rapport
30. Ask Questions & Listen
31. Provide Ideas and Advice
32. Educate on Value, Not Price
33. Increase Product Knowledge
34. Up Sell, Cross Sell, & Down Sell
35. Educate How to Buy, What to Do
36. Sell on Emotion & Dreams
37. Follow Up & Follow Up Again
38. Ask for the Sale, Confirm the Sale
39. Entertain, Wine and Dine
40. Competitions, With Follow Up
41. Make It Easy to Buy
42. Measure Conversion Rates
43. Train Entire Team in Sales/Service
44. Provide Team Incentives
45. Survey Your Past Customers
46. Survey People Who Don't Buy
47. Provide a 1st Buyers Incentive
48. Office, Vehicle & Team Appearance
49. Lighting, Clean Toilets, Air Conditioning, Kids Room, Snack Bars, & Background Music
50. Accept Trade-Ins
51. Bulk Buy Specials
52. Scarcity & Limits, Fear & Pain
53. Collect All Prospects Details
54. Stay in Touch, Cards, Newsletters
55. Give Away to Get Back, Reciprocity
56. Factory/Site Tours
57. A Gift Card Towards Purchase
58. Offer Exclusivity
59. Allow Prepayment
60. Set Sales Targets

Figure 6.1 *Ways to increase conversion rate*

My friend Bob Hill operated a Visiting Angels franchise in Connecticut. Visiting Angels is one of the many senior care franchises in a high growth but very competitive industry. When Bob took over the business, it already encompassed four territories and was doing several million dollars a year in sales. Even so there were many issues that Bob tackled one at a time and over the course of three years grew the business by more than 25 percent. He achieved those remarkable results by doing several things starting with tracking conversion rates and implementing tactics to improve them.

When Bob took over the business, the conversion rate was 46 percent, meaning 46 percent of the leads they received became clients. In a very competitive industry like senior care, that was actually pretty good. What Bob found out pretty quickly was that not all the leads were being tracked, so the conversion rate was really an unknown and likely much lower than 46 percent. The problem was that when a call came in from a potential client, it was transferred to a salesperson but not recorded as a lead in the office. Here is how Bob put it.

> And now the call gets sent to them (the salesperson). And they're in a meeting with somebody and it goes to voicemail. Or they can't take the call. It's another opportunity to lose a lead. And you think those leads got tracked? No. So this 46% very quickly probably drops down to like, 30 35%.

Bob and I spoke extensively about what he did to first ensure that every lead was tracked and second how he improved the actual conversion rate within three months from 46 percent (or something actually lower) to 55 percent. And remember this is the senior care industry, one of the most competitive industries today where a quick Google search will get you 15 franchise brands. That does not include any local independent companies out there. When someone is looking for a senior care company to help with mom or dad, all they need do is a quick search and start making phone calls. If their call is not answered or it goes to voicemail, they simply hang up and move to the next company on the list. I'll come back to my conversation with Bob shortly.

Brand Name Recognition

There is not a lot I can say here. Brand name recognition is one of the reasons you became a franchisee versus creating your own brand. Even if you are in a territory unfamiliar with your brand, you can use this to your advantage. You are part of a family that has developed the brand for you, so use that to your advantage. There is a reason that franchises do on average 1.8 times the sales of their independent counterparts.[1] Brand name recognition is one of the key reasons.

---

[1] Oxford Economics. 2021. *The Value of Franchising*, p. 5, www.oxfordeconomics .com/recent-releases/The-value-of-franchising

Build a Loyal Customer Base

Again, I wrote extensively about this in Chapter 3, so I will not repeat myself. The impact of loyal customers cannot be understated. Loyal customers buy from you exclusively and more frequently. More importantly, they become raving fans who sing your praises to everyone they know essentially becoming your marketing department.

I will not repeat the previous chapter. What I will say is that as a small business owner doing business in a local market, you must understand that word spreads quickly. A bad customer experience will not only hurt, it will linger and take a long time to overcome. Building a team of loyal customers is the best strategy for long-term sales growth because it gains you new customers with no additional marketing spend and it protects you from the occasional bad customer review. Loyal customers are more forgiving and will rally to your aid when you have that one customer who is not happy with you.

The primary benefit of building a loyal customer base is increasing your transactions. This is the number of visits or work orders or clients you visit in a period of time. Your transactions increase when loyal customers visit you or use your business more often and when they refer you new business. There are many other ways you can increase the number of transactions your business does as you can see from the following list (Figure 6.2), but building a loyal base of customers is absolutely the best and most reliable.

Pricing

Pricing is a very effective way to grow sales when done correctly. The opposite is also true, so let's talk about how to be effective with your pricing structure.

First, it is impossible to have a valid pricing discussion without including the concept of value. Too often, people equate value with low price and discounts. While that is one way to approach the value proposition, it is difficult to sustain especially during times of increasing costs. Fortunately, there is another side to the value equation that allows for higher pricing.

1. Better Service, Make Your Customers Feel Special, Give Them Magic Moments
2. Under Promise & OverDeliver
3. Streamline Your Service
4. Deliver Consistently & Reliably
5. Keep in Regular Contact
6. Inform Customers of Entire Range
7. Always have Stock
8. Offer Service Contracts
9. You Keep Client's Vital Information for Them, Develop Your Own Language
10. Product of the Week/month
11. Ask Them to Come Back
12. Use Call Cycling
13. Send Out a Newsletter
14. Run a Frequent Buyers Program
15. Create a Membership/VIP card
16. Collect a Database of Past Clients
17. Give out Members Cards or Key-Rings
18. Use a Multiple Purchase Card
19. Pre-Sell or Take Pre-Payments
20. Contracts
21. Till Further Notice Deals
22. Re-Book Next Visit Now
23. Plan Future Purchases With Clients
24. Offer on Next Purchase
25. Reminder System
26. Accept Trade-Ins
27. Increase Credit Levels
28. Offer Incentives/Rebates
29. Target likely Repeaters
30. Post Purchase Reassurance
31. Educate on Full Value
32. Suggest Alternative Uses
33. Special Occasion Cards/Gifts
34. Direct Mail Regular Offers
35. Follow Up & Follow Up Again
36. Run Competitions
37. Past Customer Events/Promotions
38. Closed Door Sales
39. Named Promotional Gifts
40. Information Nights
41. Free Upgrades for More Loyalty
42. Socialize With Clients
43. Direct Mail Special Offers
44. Catalogues so Visitors Can Re-Order
45. Cooperative Promotions
46. Keep Good Data on Clients
47. Tell Your Magic Story
48. Build a Relationship
49. Know Your Customer's Name
50. Tell them Your Full Name
51. Become Their Friend
52. Offer Free Trials
53. New Product Launches
54. Train Your Team
55. Rolling Timeline of Communication
56. Calendar Timeline of Communication

Figure 6.2 Ways to increase transactions

In general terms, value can and should be viewed as a simple mathematical equation, which describes the concept of what you pay versus what you get expressed as:

What you get – What you pay = Value

If you perceive that what you got was worth more than what you paid for it then you have received value. When I worked in restaurants, I always bought my nonslip work shoes at Red Wing Shoes. They were twice the price of nonslip shoes at Walmart but lasted more than twice as long. That's value.

This formula can be broken down by taking a more detailed look at the "what you get" aspect. When customers transact with your business, they may get any or all of the following things:

1. Product or service
2. Team member interaction
3. Environment
4. Convenience

And so, when determining what to charge for a product or service you must consider all these factors. Your franchisor will likely make pricing recommendations based on product cost, average labor, and overhead as well as what the competition charges for similar products and services. You will need to adjust those recommendations based on your costs, the sum total of what you provide, and local competition. Ultimately what your competition charges will likely be the biggest determining factor. Yes, you can charge more than your competition if you offer more so that the value equation still works in the customer's favor. For example, if you provide a guarantee when your competition does not, you increase the perceived value of your product or service.

I cannot stress enough the importance of knowing what your local competition charges, especially for products and services that are similar or the same as yours. When you go to a grocery store you will pay virtually the same price for Coke, Pepsi, or whatever other soft drink you choose, no matter which local store you visit. Check the big three fast food burger chains in your area and see what they charge for fries and drinks. You will find their prices within pennies of each other if not exactly the same. They know that for standard or basic items, they must be the same or close to their competition on pricing.

The restaurant business illustrates the concept of value better than any other industry and we have all experienced it because we all eat. There are hundreds of examples of value at both ends of the spectrum. For years, the pizza industry was dominated by local pizza shops that seldom if ever discounted. Then came Domino's that guaranteed delivery in 30 minutes or less. Price was irrelevant and quality was arguably not as good but neither mattered. The perceived value of not having to wait an hour for your pizza to arrive trumped both.

Today there are a multitude of burger franchises and the newer ones like Five Guys and Smashburger have competed very well with McDonald's, Burger King, and Wendy's by charging a lot more for a burger. They do it by providing better quality, bigger burgers, made-when-ordered, and so on. They chose to compete on the higher end of the value equation while the big three went low with dollar menus. What the big three found out was you cannot compete long-term on a low-end value strategy. The margins are too slim. Even Walmart, the perceived leader in discounting, understands this. What most customers don't know about Walmart is that they have a specific list of maybe 100 or so products that they discount at any given time. That's a very small percentage of the thousands of items they sell. Walmart knows that low prices lure customers into their stores but many of those customers end up buying a more expensive version of the product they came to buy because they perceive better value at the higher price. Of course, some customers buy the advertised low-priced item but few of them leave the store without buying something else. Contrary to popular belief, Walmart has not built an empire by selling everything at a low price.

Pricing is not just a key element of growing sales; it is also a key to growing profits. A word of caution here, you cannot raise prices indiscriminately and rarely can you raise the price of every product or service you offer all at once. Consider a slight increase on select items twice a year rather than a bigger increase once a year. The trick is to keep pace with the competition and the local economy but not get ahead of it. Remember the value equation too.

The beauty of small price increases is that they have an even bigger impact on your profit line. In fact, a 1 percent price increase can give you a 10 percent increase in profit. Suppose you sell a product for $1.00. Product cost is 40 cents, labor is 30 cents, and all your fixed costs total 20 cents. That leaves you a 10-cent profit. If you raise your price by 1 percent to $1.01, product cost is still 40 cents, it did not take any more labor to sell for a penny more so that is still 30 cents and your fixed costs remain 20 cents. Your profit is now 11 cents, which is a 10 percent increase.

Yes, this is a very simple example but it illustrates the point that a small increase in price can have a big impact on profit.

Shifting Business Mix

Unless you offer just one product or one service to your customers, your sales are generated by a menu of products or services. In many businesses (perhaps not all), each different menu item carries a different profit margin. In the restaurant business, generally speaking, higher priced menu items carry higher profit margins and dessert items are often the most profitable. Alcohol also has a high margin; however, it also is taxed more than food, which mitigates some of the margin. The point is, you need to know the margin for every product or service you sell and find ways to sell more of the higher margin items.

I have a friend Rick who owns a tavern. While his tavern is not a franchise, Rick has decades of working for several franchise brands and so learned all the lessons very well. When Rick bought his tavern, it was more of a bar that served food. Now it is a restaurant that serves alcohol. He has completely shifted the business mix and in the process doubled his average sale per customer, reduced sales tax (increased net sales versus gross sales), and increased his profit margins. Since the COVID-19 pandemic in 2020 Rick's total sales are roughly equal to prepandemic levels with half the number of customers, which has reduced the amount of labor needed dramatically. How has he done it?

The first thing he did was develop a strategy to shift his customer base. The business he bought had a deeply discounted daily happy hour. This meant that his regular customers spent a lot of time there without spending a lot of money. He pretty quickly began reducing the discounts and the number of items being discounted and shortening the hours they were offered. At the same time, he began implementing a strategy to attract customers who were willing to spend more for a better experience. In other words, offering value at the higher end of the spectrum.

Rick gradually upgraded the facilities as he could afford to do so. He did a lot of painting after hours, changed out booths for tables, changed the décor, upgraded lighting, and more. He brought in a new cook and together they developed a new menu of high-quality food with fair prices that still provided him with good margins. He added and removed items based on how they sold and made sure all the ingredients could be used in multiple items thus reducing waste. Now he has nothing on his menu that does not represent at least 4 percent of total sales.

As a franchisee, you do not have the same flexibility Rick has as an independent business owner. You cannot add and delete products or services but you do control pricing and discounts, which can accomplish similar results. Depending on your industry, how you set pricing will determine what customers purchase and how often. If you own a lawn care franchise like lawn Doctor, U.S. Lawns, or Grounds Guys, your bread and butter is services such as fertilizing, weed control, and lawn mowing. Those however are not your high-ticket items. Those are like french fries in the fast food industry. Everyone sells them so you price accordingly. Finding ways to get more custom landscaping work where people are willing to pay for high quality will shift sales and profits upward. That journey starts with knowing exactly what percent of your business each service represents and targeting your sales and marketing efforts toward the high-ticket, high-profit items.

More Stories

When I had my coaching business, I worked with a client who owned a residential alarm dealership. He was a great salesman and was excellent at training other people to sell alarm systems. He had a lot of homes with his system in them. His opportunity came on the repair and service side of the business. What was really ironic was that he knew his sales numbers but not his internal numbers like his breakeven, cost per service visit or even how many service visits he made on a weekly, monthly, or annual basis. He was solely focused on the sales side of the business because that's what he knew.

During our first meeting I was asking a lot of questions to learn as much about him and his business as possible. As I asked and he answered it came out that his contracts provided a 60-day warranty on the equipment he installed. In the first 60 days he would service the equipment and replace it, if needed, free of charge. After 60 days, the equipment was still covered but the customer paid the labor charges. That is what the contract called for but that was not what he was doing. He was not charging customers anything for the service call even after the 60-day warranty period. He was paying his people to do the work and paying the travel costs with no revenue generated. What's worse, he had no idea what this was costing him. He had a stack of service call tickets, which were used to pay his people but the stack was sitting on his very messy desk and he had no clue as to how many there were and what the total cost was. We did some analysis and found that this policy created a $12,000 loss where it should have been a $23,000 profit. So not knowing his numbers was, in effect, costing him $45,000 per year. And that was only one example of what we found in his business.

Growing Business in the United Kingdom

Stuart Allan is a business coach in the United Kingdom (UK). For years prior to becoming a coach, Stuart had a very successful manufacturing business. Now he works with business owners getting them to understand their numbers and make a lot more profit as a result. Stuart has helped hundreds of businesses become more profitable. When I spoke with Stuart, I asked him why more business owners don't pay more attention to the financial details in their business. Stuart had an interesting insight.

> So many people are scared of numbers and math and they just don't know what to charge. They don't know what to do. They have no idea about just reading business accounts. They certainly have no idea about reconciling that information, so it's complete mystery to them. They basically hand their accounts or their paperwork to the accountant once a year who produces end of year accounts. The accountant says your turnover has gone up, your profits gone up or down and your margins have changed. And that could be six nine or 12 months after year end which is absolutely meaningless.

In the UK, turnover is the word they use for sales.

I find Stuart's perspective interesting because I think there is truth in it. Stuart is not knocking or insulting anyone. He is saying that it is human nature that when we find something difficult to understand, we either avoid it or delegate it rather than dig into it and learn it. We will dig in though if we have someone to help us get through the most difficult aspect. Math is hard for some people. Financial statements are a mystery to many. As a result, many (not all) business owners do not know their numbers in enough detail to manage them and improve them in a meaningful way. Perhaps that is the number one reason the small business failure rate is so high.

Stuart has a great way of viewing business by the numbers. He is able to see things that others don't and once he points them out, they seem so obvious that people wonder why they hadn't seen it before. For example, Stuart shared a story of a hair salon owner with whom he worked. This hair salon was doing about $350,000 a year in sales. When Stuart visited the location, he immediately knew why it was not profitable. Here's how he put it:

> They were quite a small company; they were only turning over about 260,000 pounds. So that's about $350,000. And I said to them, you know, what sort of capacity do you reckon you're working at the moment? He said, Oh, God, you know, bearing in mind, we're so busy at weekends, we must be at roundabout 90 percent capacity. Well, by the time I worked out how long it took for the average hair cutting process, the number of seats they actually had in the salon, how quickly they could turn those over how many days of the week they were open, and how many hours of the day they were open, they could have actually turned over 1.3 million pounds. They had no idea.

So rather than being at 90 percent capacity, this hair salon was really at 20 percent. So, Stuart had them look at their breakeven on a daily basis and they found they made money three days a week and lost money the other days. They were not doing enough business to cover rent, utilities, and other fixed costs those days to say nothing of the labor cost. The solution was to target local marketing efforts to bring in enough business on the four slow days to at least cover costs. They launched a campaign offering special pricing during lunch and afternoon commuting hours to draw people in and began seeing results. If you have a retail business like a hair salon, restaurant, or massage studio, what is your capacity? Are you at breakeven every day? What tactics can you implement to make sure you are maximizing the capacity of your location?

The Senior Care Business

Let me get back to my friend Bob in the senior care business. Bob realized pretty quickly that while the business he had taken over was successful, there were still many opportunities to improve. In fact, by installing more discipline around the numbers or key performance indicators (KPIs) Bob increased the business by 25.7 percent in 22 months.

Bob realized there were two things he needed to start tracking more closely so he could measure the improvement. Here's how he put it.

> There's really two things that are the lifeblood of building the business. One of which is getting leads from referrals and how effective you are at converting those leads to clients. So you have to have a big pool to start with, where they're coming from. And ideally, you want about 60 percent of your leads coming from referrals. If the other 40 percent are coming from, advertising or whatever happens so that someone calls in and we say how'd you find out about us, I was Googling for homecare agency, you got a long road ahead of you to convince that person because they're talking to a number of different people. The referral one, there's a good chance that they were given a list, and you were one of three agencies that were circled as recommended so your chance at closing there is pretty good because you were referred. So you have to start out with high quality leads. Then, once you have those leads, what percentage of those do you convert? And how do you get there? So that's one component of the success. The second is actually the caregiver side and that you're able to effectively recruit caregivers, high quality caregivers with experience.

Bob told me he decided to start with the second. He began by measuring caregiver turnover overall as well as caregiver turnover in the first

90 days after they were hired. What he found was that overall turnover was below industry average at 85 percent and in the first 90 days it was double that. Hiring, orientation, and training of new team members is time consuming and expensive. It also negatively impacts the level of service the company provides its clients. By implementing a more comprehensive orientation program and a new caregiver mentoring program, Bob saw very positive results.

> So we went to 20 percent for the first 90 Day caregivers and from 85 percent overall to 40 percent overall.

Those are some very impressive results. I then asked Bob what impact that had on the business. He told me that average client retention (how long a client stayed with them) went from 9 months to 15 months. That is a 67 percent increase and a large part of why company sales increased so much. Knowing what these key indicators were, told Bob there was much room for improvement. Continual measurement allowed him to track the progress giving him important feedback on his efforts. Once the improvement is made though, the measurement must continue. If you stop measuring, you stop improving.

The other important result of reducing caregiver turnover was it allowed Bob to hire more caregivers and grow the business. So the financial benefit came not only in reducing the cost of hiring and training measured as a percent of sales, it also gave him the confidence to step up his hiring efforts, increase the number of team members, and take on more new clients. In a market where many senior care businesses stopped accepting new clients due to their lack of caregivers to serve them, Bob was able to hire and retain more caregivers and take on all the new clients other agencies could not handle. Here's Bob again:

> So now you're trying to slow the conveyor belt down. Not to the mentality when I got there which was just make the conveyor belt go faster, get more caregivers, you know, turn the thing faster. Don't worry, you have more waste. That's all right, you're hiring more. That's basically what the strategy was. And I just saw a lot of wasted time and advertising money and in my opinion, I thought

we were blowing our brand name by creating such bad will, with caregivers and clients.

I then asked Bob if they cut back on the number of orientations they conducted once turnover was under control. His response was:

Not really, because we were growing the business. We're growing the business because now we have more caregivers staying with us.

Bob attributed the fixing of this problem as a major reason why he was able to grow the business by 25.7 percent. By having a team of caregivers he could count on to show up and provide excellent care, he had the confidence to go after getting more leads and converting them to customers. He knew his team could handle the business.

To tackle the issues with the leads and conversion rate. Bob realized here that there were a couple of obstacles to overcome. Remember I quoted Bob earlier as saying that when people are calling agencies from a Google search list, having the call go to voicemail will lose the lead. The other part to that is once the call is answered, the lead needs to speak with someone knowledgeable who can answer their questions and move them to the next step in the process on that initial call. Bob's agency already had a live person answering the phone by the second ring so that piece was set. Unfortunately, when the person answering the phone transferred the lead to a salesperson, it often went to voicemail at that point. Bob changed that process.

The new process had the salespeople focused completely on referral leads. In the senior care business referrals come from hospitals, rehab centers, and assisted living facilities. Bob took the responsibility of telephone leads away from the salespeople allowing them to focus completely on those three referral sources. He then took his field team leaders, his Directors of Client Care, and trained them how to take a telephone lead call. He figured that since they were the most knowledgeable about the care giving process, they were the perfect people to answer questions and relate to the caller's needs. He taught them how to move the caller to the next step in the process (an in-home assessment) and then close the deal. Since these leads were the ones they had been losing most often, this process was responsible for the conversion rate increase to 55 percent.

Bob tracked the percent of leads that moved to an assessment, the percent of assessments that became clients and of course, the overall conversion rate, and he did this for each Director of Client Care. That way he could provide individual coaching and mentoring as needed.

As for the salespeople, Bob began measuring how many visits they made to each facility in their area and how many clients came from those visits. He found that in some cases salespeople were making a lot of visits to certain facilities without gaining many clients. Here's Bob again:

> So, when you start looking at where your referrals are, and where you're going, and how often you're going and you look at the cases that you're getting, you start drawing some conclusions as to places you need to visit less, and places you need to visit more. One salesperson was constantly in the assisted living facilities. There was an inordinate amount of business we had in assisted living facilities in that area versus another area because that's the place that he went all the time. The other guy spent a lot of his time going to the rehab centers, and hospitals. Now as I started showing, and saying, Look, you went to this assisted living facility 10 times this month. And you got one case, you went to the hospital four times this month, and you got four cases. Why don't we peel back on the assisted living facility? And why? Because there's a point of diminishing returns. If you say the hospital, you went four times, you got four cases, okay, you went six times next month, and you got six cases. I'm going to go eight next month, I went eight times, I got six cases, okay. Maybe the magic number is six.

Without tracking the numbers there is no eliminating wasted time and increasing conversion rates. That's what was happening before Bob got there. No one was tracking these numbers so there was no way to know what was really happening. All they knew was they were not getting more leads. They had no idea why or how to fix the problem.

The Case for Inventory Management

This story is from around 1990 and it amazes me to this day. I was a field rep. for Dunkin' working with franchisees in my markets to build sales and profits. I had been in the job a little more than a year when I noticed something strange with a franchisee who opened his store a few months before I arrived. Franchisees were supposed to send me their P&Ls every month so I could review with them opportunities to improve. This franchisee did not have monthly P&Ls. He did not want to pay his accountant to provide them. I used a combination of persuading him that I could help him make more money if I had his P&Ls to analyze for opportunities and reminding him that providing them to me was not optional. He finally began sending them each month.

When I did get them, I noticed immediately that food cost was high. While food cost is different in every restaurant based on pricing, product mix, and inventory management, it should be within a fairly small range when compared to other locations. His was not even close. It was off by 7 percent at least. Based on his sales, he had an opportunity to improve profits by $60,000 annually. That's a lot of money even today and in 1990 it was huge.

I began the conversation by asking to look at his inventory sheets. He told me he did not do inventory except once a year so his accountant could do an accurate tax return. His monthly food cost was based on what he purchased. When I asked him how he knew what to purchase he said he just knew what he used. I quickly figured out that he had no idea what was happening in his store even though he was there every day. For his food cost to be that high he either had a lot of waste or he was making product for which sales never made it into the cash register. I told him we could figure it out by taking inventory weekly and getting a handle on exactly what was happening. Here is the amazing part of the story. This franchisee told me that was too much work and he was not willing to do it. Not even for $60,000 a year. He could have hired someone for half that amount and still been ahead but he did not want to go through the hassle. At first, I thought he really didn't care about making more money. After a while I realized he probably was making it and didn't want me snooping around his business figuring out what he was doing. He did not last much longer. He sold his store.

I am not naïve enough to think that franchisees do not run costs through their business that are not exactly business related in order to lower their taxes. The other side of that is lower taxes requires lowering profits. That, in turn, reduces the value of the business, which impacts the ability to sell it one day and the amount a buyer will pay. More on that in the last chapter. For now, my advice is to maximize the profitability of your business by knowing where every dollar goes and find other ways to reduce your tax bill.

Understanding the numbers that drive your business is another important piece to realizing your WHY. Analyzing your P&L every month is only the beginning as you have seen from the examples in this chapter. If you are not sure what the critical ratios and numbers are in your business and the examples here have not helped you, find someone who can help you figure it out. Talk with other franchisees in your brand. Ask your franchise field rep. Hire a business coach or call me. My number is at the end of Chapter 9. Do whatever it takes and do it now. Profits are what fuels you getting to your WHY. You can't get there with an empty tank.

CHAPTER 7

Building a Relationship With Your Franchisor

We cannot control a relationship. We can only contribute to a relationship. All relationships, business or personal, are an opportunity to serve another human being.

—Simon Sinek

I have heard franchising described in many ways. Words such as marriage, partnership, contractual relationship, and legal arrangement have been used by various people I have encountered. The reality is, franchising is a relationship no matter how you term it. Like any relationship, there are some things that are clearly defined and others that reside in a gray area, which need to be worked out as they occur. The difference in franchising is that the franchisor has multiple similar relationships and must think about how each decision impacts all of them and not just any individual one. That makes for some tense situations and can make you as a franchisee feel like your franchisor is not supporting you.

It is incumbent upon both parties to communicate honestly, accurately, and above all respectfully. Now before you get all up in arms and think I'm saying responsible communication is all on your shoulders, I am emphatically not saying that. Your franchisor also must communicate honestly, accurately, and respectfully and if there is anyone reading this who is a franchisor or works for a franchisor company, hear that very clearly, look in the mirror and be honest with yourself. In more than 30 years in franchising, I have heard a lot of disparaging remarks aimed at franchisees during meetings and other private interactions. They were all just as wrong as a franchisee yelling and swearing at their franchise field rep. Now, back to all the franchisees who are the target audience of this writing, my focus is to help you so I will speak to your side of the relationship and hope you have chosen one of the better franchisors to be your partner.

A cold, hard reality of franchising is that franchise agreements favor the franchisor. The simple reason for that is they write the agreements and they get to choose who they invite to the party. You probably did not like everything you read in the agreement before signing it, but thought that less important than the opportunity to be successful and fulfill your purpose. Remember that down the road when you disagree with your franchisor on an issue. I'm not saying you should not stand up for yourself or passionately argue your point. I am saying that if things do not work out in your favor, don't be resentful. It will only poison the future.

When I was at Long John Silver's, I had the pleasure of working with two franchisees who formed a partnership to purchase locations in Missouri. Jim Sprick and Jim Sill are intelligent, open-minded businessmen who are driven by their core values. Jim and Jim are uniquely qualified to speak on the topic of franchisee/franchisor relationship because in addition to being franchisees of Long John Silver's they are A&W franchisees. They have different relationships with their franchisors but only because one takes a partnership approach and the other adheres strictly to the franchise agreement. Mr. Sprick and Mr. Sill had a lot to say on the topic.

Jim Sill

When we got into the business there was a totally different group running the place. Their word was good. We were collaborative, we always had the common goal to try to solve a problem, whether it's, we would help them, or they would help us to solve problems. I really feel like it was a win/win relationship. When the regime changed, it felt like it was win/lose. And then you look at the other side of the equation, and what can we do to help you? When the pandemic hit, immediately they suspended fees. They said until we figure out where we're going to be, hoard your cash, save your cash. We need you to be successful, we want you to be successful, we care about you.

Jim Sprick

Well, I'm going to go to a different view. I do think at the end of the day, when push comes to shove, you have a franchise agreement. That is the law. I mean, there's an agreement that you have to abide by. And like Jim said, there are some franchisors that will bend the rules a little bit depending on the economic struggles that they're having as a franchise. But, you know, if you put your attorney hat on which you have to as a businessperson, the franchise agreement is the law of the land.

One of the many reasons these gentlemen have such a fantastic partnership is that they bring different perspectives and respect each other's views. Both make sense in different ways. What Jim Sill is saying is that if one franchisor can seek win/win solutions, why can't the other? The answer is they can but as Jim Sprick said, they choose not to. As Simon Sinek says in the quote at the beginning of this chapter, we cannot control a relationship, we can only contribute. We can control our side but not the other. So, we need to think ahead and prepare ourselves to handle adversity without hoping or expecting our franchisor will step in. Remember Cindy Gray from ComForCare? She had great advice for avoiding this dilemma.

> When you're still early on and you still have some money in the bank, go get more money, get a lot of credit, get something that you can put away for an emergency situation. until you're in business long enough, you have your own money built up. You need to make sure you have money to fall back on, it's just also a really great security. I was able to get two lines of credit now, they're just sitting there, but it's good to know I don't have to really stress. I know I can make it through some pretty horrible times. And be okay. Especially when you know I have 67 employees right now depending on me.

Jim Sprick would agree with Cindy. Here is what he had to say on the subject.

If you get in any franchise, you better have some serious cash reserves because hopefully you don't need them but all of a sudden, a piece of equipment goes down the margins are thin, and, you know, once a piece of equipment goes down, it costs you 20 grand, I mean, you're working the next five years to make that back up. So that cash reserve is important for new franchisees.

Your franchisor is your partner in promoting the brand. They are not your financial partner.

Getting back to the subject of effective communication, keep in mind that as a single franchisee, your voice is not very loud. You can make it heard a little better if you follow the systems and run your business according to brand standards. The other thing you can do is always, no matter what the circumstances, communicate respectfully and as calmly as possible. One of the brands I worked for had a very unhappy group of franchisees. The source of their unhappiness was years of being treated with indifference and leadership who would not listen. Shortly after I joined the brand, a new CEO also joined. After giving the CEO a chance to settle in, I got him to agree to individual phone conversations with each member of the franchisee leadership. One of those members took the opportunity to yell and swear at the CEO. Not exactly the best way to endear himself and maximize the chance to get some of his concerns addressed. And yes, that actually happened. And yes, the franchisee wrote an apology e-mail after being chastised by his fellow franchisees and me.

I was very fortunate to have the privilege of working with an Arby's franchisee who understood how to promote a positive relationship with everyone on the franchisor side of the business even after having been burned by a member of the franchisor team. This franchisee came across as mild mannered, measured, and laid back. I learned that underneath all that was a competitive fire and a passion for being treated with the same respect he gave others. I was fortunate to have never gotten on his bad side but saw what happened to others who did. This franchisee is also a humble and private person, so he politely declined to be interviewed for the book, which is why he is not named.

Apparently before I began working with this franchisee, one of my predecessors did a number on him. I don't know all the details but I was told that this person exerted a lot of pressure on him to hire their spouse in a key operational role. The spouse did a poor job and had integrity issues. As is usually the case, it took a while for all this to come out and by the time it did, sales and profits suffered. Once the franchisee got rid of the spouse, it took quite a while to get the business back where it had been previously. I'm not sure if my predecessor quit or was fired. Either way, I was the next one up. When I started working with this franchisee, I had no idea that any of this had happened. No one said a word to me about it including the franchisee or anyone on his team. I found out a couple years later when the franchisee finally told me. He said he wanted me to know why it took him so long to trust me and know that I was truly trying to help him improve his business. He actually apologized for allowing his previous experience to cloud our relationship. I was shocked and told him he had nothing to apologize for. He had always treated me respectfully and while I did wonder why I struggled to make inroads with him, I understood why he was so guarded. I thanked him for sharing this with me and we had an excellent relationship after that. We accomplished a lot for his business and remain friends to this day. The point is even though he took a bit longer to trust me, he never really showed it.

Paul Reiser, the Sonic franchisee with whom I spoke, told me the best way to have a great relationship with your franchisor is to follow the franchise systems for operating your business. I agree with Paul. The first question I always got from every leader when I brought up a franchisee's name was "What kind of operator is he?" No one expects you to be perfect. They do expect that you are putting in the effort and trying your best every day. It's human nature to want to help people who show they are making an effort to succeed than to help people who are not. So do your best to follow the system and if you have ideas on how to improve the system, you will have more credibility, which will make it more likely your franchisor will listen.

Serving on franchisee councils is another way to keep up your end of the relationship. Once you get your business running pretty well, you will be a valuable asset to brand leadership and your fellow franchisees. These councils are advisory in nature although many franchisors will not move forward with major changes to policy or operating systems without approval of the franchisee leadership council.

Almost immediately after joining Long John Silver's as the Director of Franchise Operations, I discovered that there was no process for enforcing minimum standards. There was an audit tool to measure operating standards at the store level with a pass/fail system in place but there were no consequences for failing an audit. Consequences for lack of performance are an unfortunate necessity in any system as every group has above average, average, and below average performers. That last group hurts the other two groups and the brand as a whole and it is the franchisor's responsibility to hold them accountable. So, I created a process that provided for multiple audits to give those franchisees not meeting minimum standards a chance to improve. I then presented the process to the brand and franchisee leaders who approved it. I was then able to present the process to the entire franchisee community with the blessing of their leadership. It is always better to work together for the good of the brand than to dictate policy.

While I made this point earlier, it bears repeating. Franchisee councils are advisory in nature. They are not decision-making bodies. Franchisors use these councils to gain the perspective of their franchisees and as communication vehicles. Franchisees use them to influence decisions and to be at the forefront of changes in the brand. When a franchisor wants to test a new product or service, they will often go to council members first. Most franchisors want franchisees to embrace proposed changes because the franchisees see the vision. What franchisors need to remember is that franchisees see the vision more clearly when the changes are in their best interests. As human beings we tend to act in our own enlightened self-interests. As franchisees we act in the best interests of our teams and our businesses.

Stephen Robles (remember him from Chapter 1?) told me about a time early in his career when he was working for a national franchisor as a field rep. Stephen said:

> I had a boss tell me one time, Steven, if we have to have get our franchisees to do things, because of the franchise agreement, we've lost our relationship and we basically lost the battle. They should be doing it because they believe what we want to do; they believe in our vision. We have such great relationship that they're doing it because of our relationship. And he used the analogy of a marriage,

you know, if you're holding your marriage together, just because of a contract, you have lost a lot. And that stuck with me.

So, when your franchisor presents something new to you and your fellow franchisees always ask questions, don't be adversarial but be inquisitive. Ask how the change will help the brand. Ask how it will help the franchisees. Ask how it will benefit your customers. Ask how long and where it was tested and what were the results. By doing that you will be a good partner not only to your franchisor but also to your fellow franchisees.

One more thought on maintaining a good relationship with your franchisor and how doing that can benefit you as well as your brand. When I was with Arby's, I worked with a franchisee who was very creative and a self-proclaimed foodie. He loved trying new combinations of ingredients to create new sandwiches. One day I was visiting his locations and he showed me something he came up with that was very different from anything else on the menu. This was during the heyday of the dollar menus in the fast food industry. He called these sandwiches Arby's Minis. He found a slider-sized bun locally, put one ounce of roast beef on it and a slice of Swiss cheese. Then he microwaved it for seven seconds so it was served hot and the cheese was slightly melted. It was a very good product.

I asked him to put some information together and I brought my boss to the market to show him the product. We then worked with the product development people to standardize it and then the marketing department to test it in some different markets. If you visit an Arby's today, you will find that product on the menu as Arby's sliders in roast beef, ham, corned beef, and a couple of other flavors.

The point of that story is when you have a great relationship with your franchisor, great things can happen. When you work together toward a common goal, it is possible to create things that will benefit the entire brand and possibly even transform it. That was the case with McDonald's breakfast, which began with a franchisee. It was also the case with Dunkin' Donuts Munchkins. I am sure there are many other examples of which I am not aware. Can you imagine what would have happened if any of them came from that franchisee who yelled at the CEO on the phone? Would they have been given a fair hearing? Maybe, but it would have been a longer, harder road if it happened at all.

CHAPTER 8

Growth Through Expansion

For business and life, if you are not experiencing growth, you're possibly dying.

—Nkem Paul

To this point, the growth I have mentioned has been sales growth, team growth, and personal growth. For many franchisees, expansion into additional locations or territories is part of the plan. If taking on additional territory or adding locations to your portfolio is something you desire, you will get quite a bit of knowledge and advice from this chapter. In addition to helping a lot of franchisees open hundreds of new locations, I spoke with three franchisees on the subject. Each of the three have opened several new units or purchased units from other franchisees. Their experiences and insights on this topic were invaluable.

From my experience in working with franchisees on expansion, the first thing I will say is that the hardest location to open is your second location. That may sound a little strange since it can be so difficult to open location number one. When you opened your first location, you dealt with multiple learning curves. You had to learn the technical aspects of your business, how to effectively market it, how to hire effectively and build your team, how to manage the numbers and run your P&L to name a few. You also had to learn your franchisor, develop a trusting relationship with your field rep. and other people on the franchisor team. There was a lot of learning to be sure.

If you managed to effectively navigate all that learning and are ready to open your second location or take over a second territory, all the things you learned so far will be tested and your ability to execute those learnings will be taxed heavily. In short, you cannot run two locations or territories the way you ran one. With one location you are inevitably very involved with the day-to-day operation of your business. At first you were (are) the business. Until you grew it to the point where you could afford to turn over much of the day-to-day to the person you trained and developed, you made every decision and did much of the work yourself. Even after you had your team in place and you were able to back off for the most part, there were probably times when you felt it necessary to jump back in. If you followed the practices described in Chapters 2 and 3, you resisted those temptations and used them as learning opportunities for your team. If not, you probably took control temporarily to get through the crisis. You can't do that with two locations.

The first step to expanding your business is ensuring you are ready. Your franchisor, if they are smart, will have qualifications in place to make sure you don't expand before you are ready for it. I say if they are smart because I have seen franchisors who qualify franchisees for expansion and franchisors who don't, the latter group always ended up with closed locations and failed franchisees. To me that was a tragedy that was preventable. When a franchisor puts development of new locations ahead of ensuring franchisee success to the point that the field rep. advice is overruled, it sets up a high-risk scenario with the franchisee having the highest risk. The two things I suggest you do while still in the decision-making stage is first, implement what you have learned in this reading so far and two, have a frank discussion with your field rep. about your readiness to take on more locations. If you have developed a trusting relationship with your field rep., his or her advice will be invaluable.

The biggest piece of being ready for expansion is the people piece. Having leaders developed and ready to operate a new location is paramount. If your franchise is territory based like a senior care, cleaning, or other service-based franchise, you still need someone to lead client acquisition, development, and retention in the new territory. If you're thinking you will do that yourself, that's fine. Who will take over those duties in your current territory? You can't clone yourself and take on twice the workload. Many have tried and what inevitably happens is the first territory suffers. Client retention drops. Team member turnover goes up. Sales and profits decline because your focus and attention automatically go to the new territory and the first one suffers.

Leadership development is critical whether you intend to expand or not but it is especially critical if expansion is in your future. You can certainly hire experienced leaders from outside your company. Sometimes they work out. The hardest part of hiring leaders from outside is integrating them into your culture, which takes time. If you hire someone to run a new location, you typically hire a few months before the location is set to open. Culture integration takes more than a few months. You are also betting the success of your new location on someone you don't know very well yet. Wouldn't it be better to trust your new location to someone you know and trust already? Paul Reiser, the former Sonic franchisee about whom I wrote in Chapter 5, thinks it is.

> We've grown to 38 Drive ins and we had probably 30 to 35 managers that started out as a carhop or a cook and of our 10 supervisors, eight started out as a cook or carhop.

And Jim Sill (Long John Silver's and A&W) said this:

> I always had three to four managers in the pipeline. They would back up this opening and then hopscotch to the next one hopscotch to the next one. So we already have our management team in place for our next one and partly for the one after that. The one thing that I don't really want to do is given our size, I don't really want to take the chance on externals any more than I have to, I'm developing my own people so the person that's next in line is going to be the next and so on. I'm not opposed to externals with new blood, fresh perspectives but I also want to make sure each one is successful.

Sometimes you need to take a slightly different approach. Mr. Reiser told me that when they expanded into Alabama from Louisiana, they moved three supervisors who were interested in growing and eventually owning their own Sonics.

> The biggest challenge is getting people to move. And we found that when we moved to Alabama, we took three supervisors to Alabama. And we thought we were really going to grow with those guys. Well, they all got homesick, we ended up losing all

of them. So not only do we not still have him here, we didn't have him over there.

Paul told me he ended up buying an existing location in Alabama and using that as his base for developing people. Had that location not been available, Paul would have needed to look externally for management people but as you see, that was his third choice.

Sometimes you have an opportunity to provide growth for your leaders in a different way by creating a sort of two-for-one situation. Suppose you have an experienced manager in a lower volume location. You are opening a new location in an area where you believe it to be a home run. You can move your experienced manager to the new, higher volume location and promote an assistant in the lower volume unit. Paul told me he has done that and it works very well.

> If we build a new store, and we're like this store is going to be a great store, we'll take a manager from a low volume store in a small town with good operations, but the town's dying and we'll offer that to an experienced manager. We'll say, okay, we're going to give you this new store that we think is going to do gangbusters and we'll give your assistant manager the opportunity to move up and take over this store.

I have worked with other franchisees who have used this tactic as well. The experienced manager gains a new lease on life and new excitement as he or she takes over a new, higher volume location while the younger manager has a chance to show what he or she can do.

Once you have the people piece in place or are well on your way to getting your team ready to expand, the next piece happens pretty much simultaneously. For a brick-and-mortar concept you need to find the right location and secure financing. For a territory-based franchise, securing a location is not necessary unless you think you absolutely need a second office. One of the benefits of expansion in this type of business is that you leverage your existing office and staff by taking on additional territory with very little, if any, additional overhead. That's why I say securing a location is not necessary.

If you have a brick-and-mortar business, finding the right location and negotiating the terms is in some people's opinion the most important step. I spoke with a former colleague Greg Sausaman about the topic of growth. Greg and I worked together at Dunkin'. He has had a varied and successful career in franchising including being a Domino's Pizza franchisee, the Franchisor of Toppers Creamery, and now a master licensee for Starbucks. Greg has opened hundreds of locations and so is an expert on the subject. One of the first things Greg said to me when we spoke was this:

> We ideally want to keep our occupancy costs at six percent. If we have to, we'll go up to eight. But when you start getting occupancy costs at 11 or 12 percent, you're dead before you start. And so one of the things I always look at is the way we make money is at the very beginning, when we're negotiating the deal.

It is important to find the right location but it is equally important to find it at the right price. Never fall in love with a location to the point that you are not willing to walk away if you cannot get it with terms that allow you to be profitable. Whatever you negotiate in the beginning you will have to live with for years to come.

When Greg talked about occupancy costs at 6 percent he meant rent, taxes, and common area maintenance (CAM). Commercial leases are always triple net, which means you pay for everything. You pay rent, property taxes, and maintenance. In any location that is not a free-standing building, typically the property taxes are included in the CAM charges. Costs are always expressed in an amount per square foot, which allows each tenant to pay a fair share of the total based on the size of their space.

You also want to negotiate tenant improvement money commonly called TI. This is the amount of money the landlord will contribute to your construction costs to entice you to lease a space. TI money is usually allocated for items that will stay with the space after you leave, such as restrooms, HVAC (Heating, Ventilation, Air Conditioning) units, and other structural improvements.

Again, you have one chance to negotiate all this at the beginning so it has to make sense financially. Take emotion out of it and use the logical side of your mind. That's what the person on the other side of the deal is doing and if you don't do the same you put yourself at a disadvantage. As I said earlier, you cannot fall so in love with a location that you put yourself in a bad deal. Paul Reiser explained how he (rightly) handled this situation:

> We were very patient looking for the right location in Benton, Louisiana, I want this spot. Well, the guy wouldn't come down at all. It wouldn't work. So I said okay, we'll go find another spot. So we'd go look and find another spot. And maybe start building over there. Well, next year, we'd come back here. So it was the third year that I came back to the guy and I said, I come here every year to talk to you, and you won't talk. Let's make it happen I said, or I'm just going to have to walk away again and go build another Sonic. And he finally is like, okay, yeah, let's do it.

As much as Paul wanted that location, he knew it would only work when the numbers worked. You must be willing to walk away. Just because someone else might be willing to make a bad deal and take the location doesn't mean you should. Be patient. Even if someone does make that bad deal, chances are the location will be available again in a few years when they close.

Speaking of location, your franchisor has or should have criteria for defining an acceptable versus unacceptable location. Every brand I have ever worked for had minimums for residential population, daytime population, traffic counts on each side of the road and sign as well as building visibility (can you see the sign and building far enough away to make a safe turn in). Other important criteria are things like:

- Ingress and egress or the ease of getting into and out of the site. A right turn in and right turn out with a natural break in traffic like a light before the site is best.
- Second best is having a traffic light in front of the site. That provides access from both sides of the road and allows for an easier egress if the customer has to turn left.

- If the traffic light is just past your location, known as being on the short side of the light, you are better off being a little farther from the light. Being too close allows traffic to back up in front of your location when the light is red and prevent cars from getting in and out.
- For shopping center locations, always try for an end cap if it provides better visibility from the road. Some centers are shaped like an "L" with one end closer to the road.
- If the center is not "L" shaped, make sure there is a strong anchor store that will bring people to the center and try to get as close to it as possible. If people are coming for the anchor store, being next door or close makes it easier for them to visit you.
- Understand what time of day your peak time is and be on the correct side of the road. If you are a morning business, be on the going to work side.

I had a recent conversation with a friend who signed a franchise agreement with a sit down breakfast concept. He is looking for his first location. He believes he found a suitable spot. It is an end cap of an "L" shopping center and is close to the road. He will have great visibility, excellent residential population, and several other good attributes. The only concern I had was that he will be located where people live and not where they work. In fact, he will be at the beginning of a 25- to 30-minute commute. That would be fine for a takeout restaurant as people will eat their breakfast and drink their coffee during the commute. They will be less likely to eat a sit-down breakfast before their commute as they don't know what traffic will be like and risk being late for work. He will have a great weekend business but the weekday business is a question mark unless there are a lot of people working from home. Then he has the best of both worlds. Every industry and every brand has unique features, which cause the criteria for a successful location to be a little different. They key is to know yours like the back of your hand.

Once you have found the right location at the right price, there are a myriad of details to complete. Everything from financing, finalizing your lease or purchase, setting up utilities, design, and construction to ordering equipment and supplies, hiring and training your team, and setting up your grand opening. The list is hundreds of items long and since your franchisor has gone through the process several times, they should have it written down in some sort of timeline fashion. One reason you chose a franchise over going it on your own is so you would have processes to follow. Opening new locations is one of those processes. Greg Sausaman who has opened hundreds of stores as a franchisor and franchisee puts it this way:

And so hopefully, corporate will have the resources and the talent to say, Okay, here's a 1600 square foot space, it's 25 by 60 and is that layout. Then you get that laid out, and once it's laid out, you do the MEPs or mechanical, electrical plumbing plans. Then you go through the permitting process, you hire a contractor, then you build it, then you staff it, and then you open it. And so and I've got all that written down.

Greg continued with his Starbucks experience:

And then you have to go in for your POS. So, as you're opening you hope your franchisor has already set up POS with whoever it is Clover, or whatever the national brand is that they're working. Then they go in there and they say, here's your template. So what does that look like? And so I got it, that's another page and a half and if you've never done it, it's an ominous document. I think it's that way, probably with a lot of franchisors so if you're getting the POS, you have to plug in all your prices and sizes and all that.

POS stands for point of sale system. For a retail business, the POS system is critical to not only recording the sale and taking customer payment, what us old guys used to call a cash register, it tracks everything that is sold and provides reports that help control the business. It also allows team members to sign in and out and so provides labor information. What Greg spoke about was the process for ordering and setting up a system critical to operating a retail business. One of the many unexciting, possibly daunting tasks involved in opening a new business. You likely learned that opening your first location.

As you learned when you opened your first location or are learning as you currently go through the opening process, your franchisor will guide you and assist you along the way. I hope you paid very close attention to everything involved in the process because you may not get the same level of assistance as you open your next location. Many franchisors reduce their opening assistance on subsequent locations. They will provide location approval but expect you to do more of the work in finding and negotiating the deal. The franchisor will be involved in the initial layout and provide you with design specifications to make sure you meet the image requirements but they will expect that you already have an architect, a contractor, and are familiar with the construction process. They may also send people to help you train your new team prior to opening but it will likely be far fewer people than the first location because they expect you to have your own experienced people for training. What you will get is a process for doing everything you need to do. Follow it and ask questions when needed. Don't try to recreate the process. Let me tell you a story of what can happen if you do.

The franchisee involved in this story was the very successful Arby's franchisee I mentioned in previous chapters. By the time I began working with him and his team, they had almost 20 locations operating. They had experience opening restaurants. When I met this group, they had a new location being built and would be opening it in a couple of months, so I naturally initiated conversation about where they were in the process and how they planned to proceed. Even though they had done this many times, I saw this as a great opportunity to build our relationship by giving them more support than they expected.

Arby's had a written process for how to open a new location, which called for a certain number of days of preopening training. It didn't matter if it was a franchisee's first or 20th location, the process was the same. I found out, however, that somewhere along the line, this franchise group changed the process. Keep in mind, this was the same franchisee who told me that what he loved about franchising was that all he had to do was execute the process, not create it. Nevertheless, as I learned this group had a different process, I decided to let them follow it without me commenting. Maybe they had a better way.

Rather than doing any preopening training, this group took all of their district managers and several of the general managers from their other locations and had them work side by side with each new team member of the new store beginning on opening day. Other than a preopening orientation, each new team member's first shift was the day of opening and he or she had a "buddy" who was with them every minute of every shift for the first two weeks. After that, other general managers were rotated in to support the new team members for another two weeks. So, for the first four weeks of operation, the new location had all the district managers and several general managers to support it and make sure it was a successful opening.

At first, this might seem like a great idea. The new location had plenty of support, new team members were well trained and felt like they were well cared for and there were a lot of experienced people to deal with any issues that came up. Unfortunately, the impact on the other locations where the key leader was removed for weeks was not so great. I confirmed this as I visited their other locations where the general managers had been absent for two to three weeks and documented operations execution, which, while still acceptable, was well below the usual high standard for this organization.

The other issue with this opening process was the cost involved. Taking so many highly paid managers from their locations to work the new location for several weeks was a lot more expensive than paying team members for a few days of preopening training and using a small number of key team members from other locations.

When I spoke with the operations director about all this, we ended up having a great conversation about what was happening and how taking a different approach would not only save costs and not impact other locations, it would also allow them to open more locations per year and expand even faster. We agreed that it's important to not just ensure the success of every new location by opening strong and creating positive customer experiences from day one, it is important to make sure the reputation they had built through years of excellent operations not be tarnished even temporarily. When establishing any process, the impact of other processes and consequences to the business as a whole must be considered.

Fortunately, this story has a happy ending. Going forward, the district managers became responsible for new openings in their area. They were responsible for having a management team developed to move into the new location, working with that management team to hire and train the new store team and get the new location off to a strong start. They, of course, had support from the director and franchisee but it was their project to lead. It was a fantastic developmental opportunity for them and they appreciated being trusted with such a big role. By following this process, this organization built and opened four new locations and completed four more major remodels in one year. That was a huge success for a smaller organization and won them a prestigious award at the next franchisee convention. The moral of the story is that when you follow the process you can achieve great things.

If I have not been completely clear to this point, let me be so now. If you have any aspirations to expand your business into new areas or new locations, the two most important things you need to do are build a great team of people and manage your numbers. Doing these two things will ensure you grow from a position of strength. You cannot become profitable by expanding. I have seen many franchisees try and fail. You must be profitable and have a strong team to operate your new locations as well as continue to build your existing location. Your ability to receive funding for expansion will be determined by how profitable you are today as well as your ability to build a team. Finance companies familiar with the franchise industry know what the numbers should be in your industry. They can tell if your level of profitability is due to simply having a great location, your ability to manage the numbers or both. They obviously want both but will rely more on the second than the first.

For any type of retail or brick-and-mortar concept, you also want to consider owning the real estate on which your location is built. Your accountant will tell you there are many tax advantages to owning the real estate. I will tell you it will give you a lot more flexibility and could save your butt during hard times. Having equity in a hard asset like real estate during a recession has given a lot of franchisee access to cash and kept some of them in business. Paul Reiser commented on this when we spoke.

The equity we had in our buildings saved our butts. In 2008, if we hadn't had a lot of equity laying around, we would have struggled. But we were able to just stretch those notes out and refinance.

I have also worked with franchisees who built buildings big enough to have one or two additional businesses beyond theirs. That has allowed them additional flexibility by forming another company and be in the real estate business. It's not for everyone but as you will see in the next chapter, real estate adds a lot of business value and gives you options when it is time to exit the business.

Opening new locations and expanding into new territories is exciting stuff. Your team will love being part of an expanding business as it creates opportunities for them to grow and advance in their career with you. Stagnation is one of the reasons people leave a company, so the fact that you are expanding gives your team a strong reason to stay. The final reason expansion is exciting because when you do it right, it has tremendous impact on your company's value. No matter what your future plans are for your business, creating value should be at or near the top of your mind.

CHAPTER 9

Creating Business Value— Having an Exit Plan

Begin with the end in mind.

—Stephen Covey

In his book *The 7 Habits of Highly Effective People*, Stephen Covey lists the second habit as begin with the end in mind.[1] I am using the quote in my final chapter because I believe firmly that your exit plan is something that you should be thinking about from the very beginning. I don't mean that you should be thinking about selling from day one or that you should focus on whatever your end game is every day. What I do mean is that you should be making decisions every day that will build the value of your business so that when the time comes for you to execute an exit strategy, it simply becomes the next step of a plan created years before.

Covey asks his readers to imagine themselves at their own funeral. What will people say about you? His point is that whatever people say, it will be a reflection on how you lived. In the same way, the value of your business when you are ready to retire will be a reflection of how you operated it. Isn't it better to understand that concept and take action now rather than waiting until you are at or near the end?

Another way to look at this so you understand what I mean is to think of your exit strategy as two separate pieces. The first piece is to build a business that has value. Build something that someone will want to own one day. That's the part that you need to think about and act on every day starting with day one. The second part comes way down the road when it is time to execute an exit strategy. That's when you decide what the strategy will be. Will the business transfer to the next generation in your

---

[1] S. Covey. 1989. *The Seven Habits of Highly Effective People* (Simon Shuster) Chapter 2.

family? Will you sell it on the open market? Will you go public? Those are decisions for a later date. If you make that decision early on, the tendency will be to focus on that and lose sight of building something of value. You will also limit your options. The more value you build, the more options you will have for exiting.

David Shavzin is the owner of a company called The Value Track and the founder of Exit Planning Exchange Atlanta. David has worked with lower mid-market companies for more than 20 years helping them create and increase business value as part of a clear exit strategy and then taking them to market to sell. David was kind enough to speak with me and share his expertise as well as some stories. One of the first things David told me related to this twofold approach. He said:

> When I talk about exit planning in front of many of the professional advisers out there, and especially with many business owners, they are simply thinking about the transaction. Planning for the transaction is critical, but the other half of the equation is running your business well from the beginning, keeping value in mind with every decision you make. You will be way ahead of the value game when it gets closer to transaction time.

Very insightful comments from a man who has helped many business owners increase their business value and exit with much more than they otherwise would have.

And our Sonic franchisee, Paul Reiser put it this way:

> Plan your exit strategy on day one? I hear that a lot. I was watching Shark Tank the other night, and these people were starting their business, and they were talking about their exit strategy, and the sharks jumped all over their case. They want them to be all in, they don't want you thinking about exit strategy when you're creating your business. I think they want all their passion; they want all their heart; they want to make sure this person's committed. So, when I say exit strategy on day one, I'm saying build it so that it's something that somebody would want to buy. So, on day one, know that I have to have this thing in a situation where it's running itself, so that I could sell it. And what you're doing is

you're creating a successful operation for yourself, because yes, I've got to replace myself as operator. If you come in and you say, I've got to run this thing, it's not going to be as successful as a stand-alone business, and you're certainly never going to be able to sell it because if you're the reason that it's successful, nobody else is going to buy it, because it's worthless. So, on day one, make sure that you're planning on selling it. You're building it in such a way that somebody would want to buy it not because you're going to sell it tomorrow, but because if you build it that way, it's going to be more valuable for you. And eventually, someday, you'll either be able to hand it off to your kids, you'll be able to bring in a professional president or director of operations that can run it, or you'll be able to sell it.

When I tell you more of Paul's story, you will listen to him and follow his advice.

In 1977, Paul's dad Merlin moved the family to Louisiana and became a Sonic franchisee. In those days, as Paul describes it, you could pay $6,000 for a 25 percent ownership in a Sonic location. Sonic made the investment in the building and equipment and you were responsible for operating it. Over time, Merlin was able to purchase some underperforming locations outright and developed a small town strategy. As I wrote in Chapter 5, he developed his local marketing strategy that Paul continued when he took over the operation. Owning the schools, the churches, and neighborhoods in the small towns where he did business allowed Merlin to build a solid base, which Paul and his siblings built into an incredible business with tremendous value.

Paul and his sisters grew up in the business. They worked as car hops and cooks and eventually began managing locations. As his sisters got married, their husbands also began managing locations. It was a real family business. After college, Paul decided he wanted to not just work in the business, he wanted to own part of it. Here is how he tells the story.

The whole family worked in Sonics. I was a little 12-year-old car hop out there but always wanted to get away from the business. And then I'm coming back to the business. All through high school, I worked in stores and managed stores. In college, I would drive around and give managers a night off so that was kind of my job. Brothers-in-law started getting married into the family, they started running stores. So ended up I came back to work managing a drive in, bought out my dad's partner. He was just a finance guy from Kansas. And he was very gracious and let me buy him out. And so, we realized that man, we were growing slow. So, let's form a management company. You see what we would do is I'd say Dad, I want to build a Sonic here. He'd say build it. So, he'd own half and I'd own half but it took a long time and it was hard to do. And my other brothers-in-law each did the same thing. So, there were five of us in the business and we each had a Sonic with my dad and he then had some other partners. So we formed a management company in 2003. And we just started building Sonics. And that's when we got our development agreement for Alabama. And so we went from 13 stores to 38 stores in 10 years after that.

Opening 25 restaurants in 10 years is no easy feat. Finding the right location, financing it, building it, developing the management team, and getting it open is a long, involved process as you learned in the last chapter. What are some of the details that allowed Paul and his partners to accomplish this?

There's a lot to be said, for pulling together. There's a lot to be said for realizing that 20 percent, of 30 stores is better than 50 percent of one store or two stores. Especially when you get the economies of scale and you start bringing in supervisors.

Paul and his partners built a valuable business not just to sell it one day. They built it for many reasons. They wanted to build a business that would support their families in a comfortable lifestyle. They built it because they wanted to create opportunities for others to support their families. They built it because they enjoyed the process and could be proud of what they accomplished. They built something that had value to them and as it turns out had value to others.

Paul continued:

So that was our plan early on. We said, we know that either the next generation is going to take over, or we're going to have to run it as a board of directors with a management team that manages it, or at some point, we're going to sell it. So day one, make it duplicatable, and make it sellable, valuable. A second strategy, I would say is, before you ever open your first drive in or restaurant, or whatever the franchise is, most people have some type of partners. It would be very rare that one person would just walk in and say, I'm going to be a franchisee on day one, because franchisors one, they want you to have money, or experience or both. So most people who have enough money don't want to run it. Like if I buy a franchise, I'm not going to go run it right now. But most young hungry guys that want to go run it, but they don't have money. So you're going to have a partnership. So from day one, set up your partnership in a way that you know what the exit would look like. It's so much easier when you're excited and when you haven't made any money, and when no one has any blood or sweat equity in it to decide objectively, okay, 10 years from now, what would it take to sell it? So let's set it up. If there's three of us, majority automatically rules, right? Majority rule, we're going to sell it or we're going to keep it and make sure that your Articles of Incorporation are set up and they say it that way.

Paul had a third piece of advice:

Don't cut any corners along the way. We had three stores with slight encroachments. Make sure that your plats are right, that you're set within your boundaries and that everything's tightened up, because out of sight, out of mind. But 30 years from now, when you go to sell this thing or 10 years, or five years, or one year, the person that's buying it from you, that'll put a red flag up. One of the properties we owned we still have not been able to sell because we are still correcting title on it. They'll buy it eventually but we're spending a lot of money.

So Paul and his partners, by beginning with the end in mind, did a lot of things right along the way and were able to exit when they wanted to exit, as you will see. On the other hand, David Shavzin told me stories of clients who brought him in to help them exit and found they were not ready.

We talk specifically about transferable value, which is really a key starting point. We provide a lot of education for owners, critical when they have not been through this before. It covers a range of topics. Owners tend to think when revenue is doubling or even tripling, that it means the company is more valuable. But if profitability is going down, revenue doesn't matter. Revenue, in a vacuum, is not the answer. The key is understanding what somebody will pay for it. I've built this thing for 30 years, my blood sweat and tears, and so on. But that doesn't mean there's been a focus on building value. So the first question we answer what it's worth today. Get a sense of that. Everyone on the same page. Often owners can be disappointed but this is the reality. The next question is what to work on to build value? What's my new target date to get out and new target value? Can I wait and work on this for two or six years? With those questions answered, we can start to diagnose and prioritize. Whatever their new timeframe, there might be 100 things they could do, and should do. So we have to force a prioritization based on their now new goals. In the case of one client, the priorities at the beginning were a brand overhaul, including a new website, rebuilding the entire marketing machine, and working with everybody in the company to help align individual roles with critical company objectives. In other cases, a software implementation to improve operations rose to the top. At the end of the day, the buyer wants to walk in and find the owner to be just about irrelevant. A buyer wants to see that everything is working stunningly well and they can just "get a check every month." In summary, we have to start there, and prioritize. We look at everything you can possibly imagine that goes on inside of a company, from marketing to IT to supply chain to risk management and human capital. We wrap our heads around it and say here's what we think we've got to do, and can do, in the time leading up to our new deadline. At this point, they are so much more valuable when we go to market to sell the company.

As you see, the consequences of not following Paul's or David's advice can be significant. You will either get significantly less than you thought when you sell or you will need to pay someone like David to help you fix things and delay your exit for as long as it takes to accomplish those tasks. David will probably not like me saying this but it makes much more sense to begin with the end in mind and follow the principles I and my contributors have mentioned, so you don't need to hire him and delay your exit. Although David did tell me that he has worked with clients who followed his advice and implemented his recommendations and decided not to sell their business. One of his clients reduced his work week from 80 hours to 40 hours and was able to keep the business and still spend more time with his family. He will exit one day but meanwhile he has the best of both worlds.

So now you have this business and things are going well. You defined your purpose, built a team you can count on to run the day-to-day operation, you have a system in place for prioritizing and achieving goals every 90 days, you have a loyal customer base and a stellar reputation in all your local markets, your numbers are tight and your team knows how to keep them that way, you have an excellent relationship with your franchisor and you have grown to at or near capacity in your assigned territory. Maybe you are now thinking it's time to move on to the next challenge or cash out and live on a tropical island somewhere. It doesn't matter what your motivation is, you have begun thinking it may be time to exit. How do you know when it's time? As with everything else, this is not a decision to make quickly. The correct answer will reveal itself over time.

Over the number of years you have your franchise, you will interact with your franchisor and other franchisees perhaps hundreds of times. During those many interactions, you will hear about locations for sale or ones that just sold among lots of other things. You may ask your franchisor if there are any locations for sale that make sense for you to acquire. You may also attend franchise industry trade shows and other events that allow you to meet franchisees from other brands. Through all these interactions, you will begin to get a sense of how much your franchise is worth. You will begin to understand that well-run franchises sell for more and poorly run franchises sell for less. You will learn what buyers want and what they are willing to pay for. Even if you are still years away from thinking about exiting, pay attention. Knowledge is always a good thing to have. That's what Paul Reiser did.

We've built relationships with franchisees small and large over the years and you always hear when somebody sells something. Sonic corporate is very good, your franchisor is very good at knowing valuations. So over the years we wanted to buy something we said anything in this area that comes available we would like to buy it. That's a good way to find out the valuations. You've always got your ear to the ground, you're involved with the franchise organization, you're involved with other franchisees and like, oh, a Sonic just sold what did it sell for? What was the multiple? How did it work?

Paul continued:

So, if a guy one county over is ready to retire and his kids aren't going to take over he wants to sell. You say well Sonic what's the word? What's a Sonic worth these days and it just kind of came to the point where it was worth a multiple of earnings. You look at your net bottom line and for years and years it was five times earnings because Sonic was a good company. Then in 2008, if you could sell one, you might get three times earnings, but you probably couldn't sell it. So that was kind of the bottom. As long as we've been involved, it's got as high as five and a half times earnings. And this is again mainly just hearsay. Other franchisees tell you that's what it sold for. So the business would be five and a half times net profit and then you just get an appraisal for the real estate and real estate might just be a multiple of rent.

To paint a clearer picture, while Paul and his partners were actively growing their business opening new locations and buying one here and there, they were also keeping an eye on what was happening on the exit side of the business. Even when they were not thinking of selling, they still had a pretty good idea of what their business could be worth on the open market. They would tuck this information away until the day they were ready to use it. As Paul told me:

So in my mind, I wanted to have this thing paid off, and have our sales up to X million. And then, with five partners, we'd all do pretty good. So that was kind of my thought in the back of my mind. So five years from now, we're going to have a hard look, at selling this thing, because everybody's going to be well into their 60s, I'm going to be at 59, the youngest and I don't want to run this thing by myself. There's only one grandson that was kind of interested so it really didn't look like it was going to be a transition to the next generation. But again, you hear Sonics sell, what's the valuation. We didn't have a chart that we read every month. It's just a kind of a close association with people and, you know, we just got hundreds of friends in the Sonic business.

The size of your company defined by sales and profits will obviously determine how much you can sell it for. Again though do not forget that how you set it up will also be a big factor. All things being equal, a company set up to run without you will be worth more than one where you are a key piece of the operation for reasons explained earlier.

The size of your company will also determine the options available to you when it comes time to sell. For example, if your company is one location doing five million in sales with a 10 percent profit, your options may be limited to individuals who want to be first-time business owners and other franchisees of your brand. If however, you have grown your company to multiple locations with tens of millions in sales and profits, you can add private equity firms and venture capitalists to your list.

Most franchises sell for a multiple of EBITDA, which stands for earnings before interest, taxes, depreciation, and amortization. It is simply a measure of profitability that removes items from the equation, which will inevitably be different for the buyer than they are for you. It also allows buyers to evaluate different deals on a level playing field to determine which one is the best. Usually businesses sell for a multiple of EBITDA. That multiple changes based on market conditions that determine for the buyer, which investments are more attractive. The key thing to remember here is your business is not worth what you want for it; it is worth what someone is willing to pay for it. The market will give you a starting point, but ultimately the price will be adjusted up or down based on the number of interested parties and what they offer you.

When the stock market is good, investors will put their money into stocks because that's where they will earn the highest return until the market goes so high that the risk becomes too great. When interest-bearing investments like bonds are doing well, the money will go there. When those types of investments are not as good, investors will look for profitable businesses that are run like Paul and his partners ran their Sonics. A business where the buyer can come in and replace the owners and not have to be involved in the day-to-day operation. When those market conditions exist, companies like Paul's become much more valuable and the EBITDA multiple goes up. That is exactly what happened with Paul's Sonics.

I also get tons and tons of offers in the mail for you know, would you like to buy a Sonic? Or would you like to sell a Sonic? So every once in a while, I'd take a peek at those and I built relationships with different brokers. And I got to talking with this guy. And he started telling me that because the interest rates had just tanked forever all of a sudden you got equity firms that are interested. And so now because the stock market's through the roof, and the bonds are through the floor, and interest rates are low, all of a sudden, these equity firms said, well, we want to buy a nice midsized group of predictable sales and profits. And Sonic is good long term, they've got good valuations and here's a good company. Well, if we're going to get into Sonic and I'm an equity firm, I don't want to buy two Sonics. I don't want to build a Sonic; I want to buy a footprint that's in a core market. Nobody sells good Sonics; you can only buy bad Sonics. So because we are good Sonics and we're in a core market, all of a sudden, these equity firms are willing to pay this premium because of what we have. Prominent locations, a business that we have set up from the beginning, that we have got management in place, real estate in place and sales and profit. So here it is we're able to sell it to someone who just wanted to do investment dollars and didn't want to run it. All of a sudden, three years ago, the guy tells me it's worth so much more multiple than we've ever looked at.

You've heard the phrase timing is everything? That's not really true. What is everything is setting up your business so it runs without you.

That way you can be patient and wait for the timing to be in your favor. That's exactly what Paul and his partners did. Paul finished the story this way:

> So we said we'll go do some real numbers on this. So, we paid and we had appraisals of all the properties done. But also, we went and met with different brokerages, we do all our banking with Regions Bank, and they have a branch that's just a big brokerage firm, so them and two others, we just kind of said here's what we have just kind of give us an evaluation. And they came back with a really high number and we're like, okay, we've got to take this seriously. So now all of a sudden we're looking at these valuations that are really high and we're at a place in our in our career where everyone's maybe looking at retiring in the next five or eight years. But if we wait five years are things going to turn? And we also knew Biden was running for president and he had put out his tax plan doubling capital gains from you know, 20 to 39 and a half, right? All sudden, we're like, if we wait five years, we have to double our capital gains, that just kind of put a little bit of a time pressure on it. So we just decided that this was time. So we went through the whole process with the brokerage, and they basically said, you've got five partners so what's the number that you will take? And we came up with our numbers and said if we can get this range, then we'll vote again. Then we went through the long process of working with a broker. What they did was they put together a nice package, they sent out to 250 targeted prospects that here we have 38 drive ins and the core market. If you're interested in signing a nondisclosure agreement, then we'll send you the package. So it took months to put together this package that was about 100 pages that really broke down our business. Out of 250 we got 40 responses. Of the 40 responses, we got 25 offers. We took the top 10 and then we went into serious negotiating meetings. Then we got this really nice offer and then Sonic exercised their right of first refusal.

Many franchisors have a clause in the franchise agreement giving them the right of first refusal on the sale of any franchise. That means essentially that since they need to review and approve the sale anyway, if they like the deal, they can purchase the business under the same terms. You as the franchisee do not lose anything except the few weeks it takes your franchisor to make a decision. If your locations are near or adjacent to locations operated by your franchisor, there is a higher likelihood of this happening. Sometimes the deal is just too good for them to pass up.

For every story like Paul's where after years of operating a successful franchise business he and his partners sold it for enough money to let them retire in comfort, there are stories of franchisees who have not been so fortunate. I have seen franchisees who sold their business for far less than they initially thought it was worth. I think it is very sad to see a franchisee work hard for years thinking their business will fund their retirement plans only to have the opposite happen. Don't let that happen to you.

Follow the advice you read about in these pages. I have intentionally included advice and quotes from franchisees in addition to sharing my own. I did that because there is strength in numbers. Your success is too important to me to entrust it to my advice alone. While I know my advice is sound, you don't know me and so have reason to doubt. I hope that by including the words of other successful franchisees it has served to strengthen my words enough for you to heed them.

I wish you every success in the world. I want you to build a legacy for you and your family that will serve whatever purpose you chose in the beginning. If you find yourself in need of more help than I have provided in these pages, please feel free to contact me. You can find me on LinkedIn or just e-mail me at djroemer110@gmail.com or call me at 740-972-9841.

Health, Happiness, and Success are yours for the taking. Always remember to enjoy the journey!

About the Author

Dave Roemer is a more than 30-year veteran of the franchise industry. The majority of his career he has worked with franchisees of Dunkin' Donuts, Arby's, TGI Friday's, Long John Silver's, and Einstein/Bruegger's/Manhattan Bagel as an operations and business consultant. In these roles, he was able to work side by side with hundreds of franchisees and operators to grow their sales and profits as well as develop their teams. He is a natural trainer and coach who believes strongly that people respond to positive reinforcement and redirection rather than an authoritative style.

After years on the franchisor side of the business, Mr. Roemer decided to put his money where his mouth was and became a franchisee of a worldwide small business coaching franchise. That experience allowed him to expand his knowledge beyond the restaurant industry and into businesses of all kinds. He describes it as the greatest learning experience of his life.

Because of his experience as a franchisee, Mr. Roemer is now combining his desire to help franchisees achieve their dreams with his desire to help anyone interested in franchise ownership find the best franchise opportunity for them. He considers it his mission in life to help people join great brands and avoid those who are not best in class. Once he helps you find your "right fit franchise" he can help you become a hugely successful franchisee.

Dave is available to speak to franchise groups at regional and national meetings as well as to students in entrepreneurship programs and groups of small business owners of all kinds.

Index

OTHER TITLES IN THE ENTREPRENEURSHIP AND SMALL BUSINESS MANAGEMENT COLLECTION

Scott Shane, Case Western University, Editor

- *Building Business Capacity* by Sheryl Hardin
- *The Startup Master Plan* by Nikhil Agarwal and Krishiv Agarwal
- *Managing Health and Safety in a Small Business* by Jacqueline Jeynes
- *Modern Devil's Advocacy* by Robert Koshinskie
- *Dead Fish Don't Swim Upstream* by Silverberg Jay
- *The 8 Superpowers of Successful Entrepreneurs* by Marina Nicholas
- *Founders, Freelancers & Rebels* by Helen Jane Campbell
- *Time Management for Unicorns* by Giulio D'Agostino
- *Zero to $10 Million* by Shane Brett
- *Navigating the New Normal* by Rodd Mann
- *Ethical Business Culture* by Andreas Karaoulanis
- *Blockchain Value* by Olga V. Mack
- *TAP Into Your Potential* by Rick De La Guardia
- *Stop, Change, Grow* by Michael Carter and Karl Shaikh
- *Dynastic Planning* by Walid S. Chiniara

Concise and Applied Business Books

The Collection listed above is one of 30 business subject collections that Business Expert Press has grown to make BEP a premiere publisher of print and digital books. Our concise and applied books are for...

- Professionals and Practitioners
- Faculty who adopt our books for courses
- Librarians who know that BEP's Digital Libraries are a unique way to offer students ebooks to download, not restricted with any digital rights management
- Executive Training Course Leaders
- Business Seminar Organizers

Business Expert Press books are for anyone who needs to dig deeper on business ideas, goals, and solutions to everyday problems. Whether one print book, one ebook, or buying a digital library of 110 ebooks, we remain the affordable and smart way to be business smart. For more information, please visit www.businessexpertpress.com, or contact sales@businessexpertpress.com.

CPSIA information can be obtained
at www.ICGtesting.com
Printed in the USA
JSHW062140100822
29135JS00006B/191